# TEN
# TELECASTER
# TALES

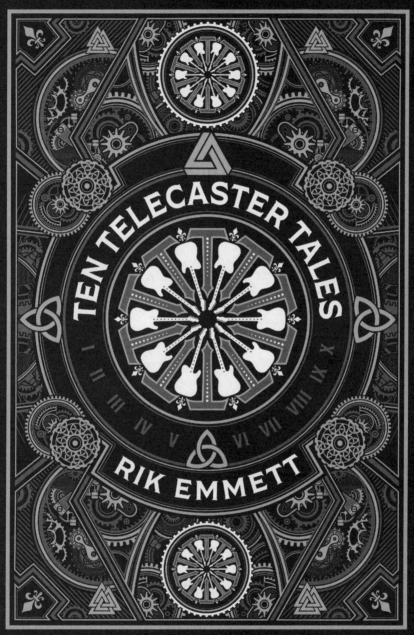

# TEN TELECASTER TALES

## RIK EMMETT

LINER NOTES FOR A GUITAR AND ITS MUSIC

Published by ECW Press
665 Gerrard Street East
Toronto, Ontario, Canada M4M 1Y2
416-694-3348 / info@ecwpress.com

Editor for the Press: Michael Holmes /
a misFit Book
Copyeditors: Lesley Erickson and
Sammy Chin
Illustrations: Jeanine Leech
Photos: Rik Emmett
Text design: Jennifer Gallinger
Cover design: Jeanine Leech

MISFIT

LIBRARY AND ARCHIVES CANADA CATALOGUING
IN PUBLICATION

Title: Ten Telecaster tales : liner notes for a guitar
and its music / Rik Emmett.

Names: Emmett, Rik, author

Identifiers: Canadiana (print) 20240485831 |
Canadiana (ebook) 2024049847X

ISBN 978-1-77041-826-4 (softcover)
ISBN 978-1-77041-827-1 (hardcover)
ISBN 978-1-77852-385-4 (ePub)
ISBN 978-1-77852-386-1 (PDF)

Subjects: LCSH: Emmett, Rik. | LCSH: Guitarists—
Canada—Biography. | LCSH: Composers—
Canada—Biography. | LCSH: Rock musicians—
Canada—Biography. | LCGFT: Autobiographies.

Classification: LCC ML419.E54 A3 2025 | DDC
782.42166092—dc23

This book is funded in part by the Government of Canada. *Ce livre est financé en partie par le gouvernement du Canada.* We acknowledge the support of the Canada Council for the Arts. *Nous remercions le Conseil des arts du Canada de son soutien.* We would like to acknowledge the funding support of the Ontario Arts Council (OAC) and the Government of Ontario for their support. We also acknowledge the support of the Government of Ontario through the Ontario Book Publishing Tax Credit, and through Ontario Creates.

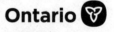

PRINTED AND BOUND IN CANADA          PRINTING: FRIESENS     5   4   3   2   1

Purchase the print edition and receive the ebook free.
For details, go to ecwpress.com/ebook.

———◆——→

*To Smitty and Garren,*
*who helped me dream up the Telecaster named Babs.*

*And to all the Telecaster players on the planet.*

*But most of all,*
*to the ones who made me dream about*
*what a Telecaster could do.*

*In order of appearance in my life:*

*Robbie Robertson, Domenic Troiano,*
*Steve Cropper, Roy Buchanan.*

*The Yardbirds alumni —*
*Eric Clapton, Jeff Beck, and Jimmy Page.*

*Ed Bickert, Ted Greene, Danny Gatton,*
*Bill Frisell, and Julian Lage.*

*And — as always — to Jeannette Ann Bernadette,*
*who knows the story behind all the stories*
*of the storyteller.*

←◆——→

# Contents

———●———

TABLE OF ILLUSTRATIONS      XI

    BY JEANINE LEECH


PART ONE — PREAMBLE

  1. THE REAL MAGIC OF LAYERS      3

  2. THE STORIES WITHIN THE STORIES WITHIN      6
       *THE* STORY

  3. YOU GOT TO MOVE IT, MOVE IT      10

  4. TELECASTER — IN PURSUIT OF THE TRUTH      13

  5. THE TELL-TALE TELECASTER (A POEM)      20

  6. THREE YEARS IN THE MAKING      23

  7. ELI'S LOFT      28

  8. BACKGROUND AND FOREGROUND      33

  9. PERSPECTIVES ON THE GUITAR — DEFYING      41
       THE ODDS

10. ARCHETYPES AND POETIC FAITH      46

11. OUTSIDE IN, INSIDE OUT      52

12. MY WHEELHOUSE AND MY WOODSHED      55

13. LAYERS      60

14. THE TIGHTROPE WALKER'S SEARCH      66
       FOR BALANCE ("BOTH SIDES NOW")

15. TRYING TO FIND THE RIGHT MIX FOR THE TALES      73

16. WHY BOTHER?      77

17. WHY TEN?      80

18. THE ABIDING GRACES     83

19. SPACE     91


PART TWO — TEN TELECASTER TALES

  1. SO PUSHY     105

  2. FUNKY SCRATCHIN'     115


*THE BARN DANCE SUITE*

  3. SWIRLING (COURANTE)     120

  4. ALLEMANDE     126

  5. COWBOY AND GAUCHO WALTZ     135
     (VALSE A RASGUEADO)


  6. SLINKY     140

  7. BURLYTOWN     146

  8. THE RIO GLIDE     154

  9. GEE WHIZ     159

  10. WINTER NOCTURNE     164


*"THIS KIND"*     179


ADDENDA

  1. MIX NOTES FOR *Ten Telecaster Tales*     181
     BY BLAIR PACKHAM, PROJECT ENGINEER

  2. MASTERING NOTES FOR *Ten Telecaster Tales*     188
     BY STEVE SKINGLEY


SPECIAL THANKS     193

# TABLE OF ILLUSTRATIONS

## By Jeanine Leech

———◆———

| | |
|---|---|
| PORTRAIT OF THE AUTHOR WITH ELI | VII |
| DREAMS TAKE FLIGHT | 5 |
| PATENT DRAWING | 9 |
| CASTLE IN THE CLOUDS | 12 |
| CHROME MANDALA | 19 |
| CLOCKWORKS | 23 |
| MY LIBRARY WINDOW | 29 |
| ELI THE WONDER HORSE TAKES FLIGHT | 29 |
| DEAR DIARY | 35 |
| A PORTRAIT OF SOME NAKED TRUTH | 38 |
| DEFYING THE ODDS | 45 |
| SILVER MAPLE TREE | 47 |
| GUITARIST INSIDE OUTSIDE PRINCIPLE | 54 |
| WHEELHOUSES IN THE WOODSHED | 59 |
| TRIANGULATIONS | 60 |
| FLEUR-DE-LYS | 65 |
| TIGHTROPE WALKER | 71 |
| EYE AND EAR | 76 |
| RUBBER STAMP | 82 |
| TRIANGLES OF SPIRITUALITY | 90 |
| MANDALA AND STARS | 94 |
| CELTIC KNOT | 101 |

# Part One

## Preamble

# 1

# The Real Magic of Layers

◆—▶

Magicians swear an oath to maintain their illusions, never revealing the secret of the trick, allowing the delicious mystery to work its spell upon the audience.

That's not in my nature.

Despite an entire adult life spent professionally in show business, I quickly lose interest in the insecurities that lead to trumped-up con jobs. I'm not keen on perpetuating fraud. For me, sweet reward comes with *revelation*. Discovery. Understanding. I like stories that pay off by making sense, resonating with truth.

I think that's why music making's strongest attraction for me — particularly music in song form — is that its nature maintains the integrity of a true mystery. One plus one can somehow equal three, so the process of composing, combining one idea with another, keeps adding something extra. Then, miraculously, the performance of a piece of music (sometimes even the recording of it, when you manage to get it right) can add *more* layers of magic to the equation.

It doesn't end there. It turns out that circumstances, environments, and the passage of time generate extra layers of supernatural mystique. I don't think "supernatural magic" arises from anywhere except our human imagination — but I do believe our imaginations are infinitely elastic. As a result, music keeps changing, revealing itself in different ways. Bearing witness to this throughout the creative act — being present as this evolution is happening — adds yet another personal layer, because all my experience has made me acutely aware that this feature of the process, this particular chemistry of the moment, is unique to everyone. And yet — while this evolution of the moment is personal — we're also *sharing* it.

Communion.

That's some *real* magic right there.

*Dreams Take Flight*

# 2

# The Stories Within the Stories Within *the Story*

———◆———

THE STORIES IN THIS BOOK ALL BEGAN WITH ONE STORY, which began very practically: *design a guitar.* I was committed to a casual and logical long-term development plan that aimed for the hardware to meet the software of my soft machine. The original question was, could one guitar embody the ergonomics of a lifetime spent developing my preferences?

I conceptualized, then consulted with Mike "Smitty" Smyth, the guru of MJS Custom Pickups in Mississauga. My aesthetics of simplicity still mandated enough design features to provide for a range of sounds I would be requiring for tasks that lay just beyond the horizon.

My main concern was ergonomic comfort. Smitty then curated the design of a hybrid electric guitar — a Telecaster shape and style, with a Les Paul's scale length, bridge height, and neck angle, sporting a Stratocaster's bar-of-used-soap body sculpting.

Approaching my seventieth birthday, I played seated more often than standing, so this imagined guitar needed to float on my thigh — no more than seven pounds. The perfect instrument would feature Smitty's new zero-hum pickup design, offering a lower output, which yielded a more articulate range of character in its voice.

We took on a teammate. As curator of the project, Smitty recommended Garren Dakessian of Loucin Guitars in Oakville, Ontario, as our custom builder/luthier. The original construction took several months; subsequent tweaks and modifications lasted even longer. As I became more intimate with the aesthetics and subtleties of the guitar, it eventually took on top-of-the-line locking tuners and a black pickguard.

A romantic historical notion concerning Fender Telecasters is that the playing of Roy Buchanan originated the historic obsession with "blackguards," a single-ply black Bakelite pickguard on a butterscotch finish. In turn, Keith Richards and Bruce Springsteen did their own things to enhance and perpetuate that romantic infatuation. I concur.

But the list of Telecaster champions is long, and my own story about the guitar would not be complete if I didn't include Ted Greene, Ed Bickert, and more modern standard-bearers like Bill Frisell and Julian Lage. More on them in a bit.

As any lifer musician will tell you — new gear can be very inspiring. At the very least, it helps you time-travel back to your youth, when new gear was lusted after and highly cherished. Still — bonding with my new instrument took over a year. During that time, the prevailing question became, what kind of music might this new guitar facilitate?

I began composing and learning the pieces that comprise the Ten Telecaster Tales.

In the fall of 2023, I finally settled on the guitar's nickname: Babs.

Firstly, it's an acronym — **B**lackguard **and B**utterscotch. Secondly — for a while, I'd been calling her "Butter" (for the colour of the finish on the swamp ash body), which morphed into "Buttah," pronounced like Mike Myers's SNL character, Linda Richman, in describing Barbra Streisand's voice.

Streisand's nickname? *Babs.* (I'm a big fan. Such a voice.)

So, there it was. *Had* to be.

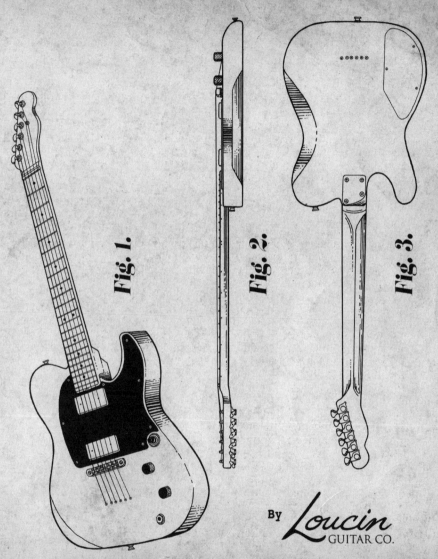

Fig. 1.

Fig. 2.

Fig. 3.

By *Loucin* GUITAR CO.

Garren Dakessian / luthier
Mike 'Smitty' Smyth / designer, curator
Rik Emmett / designer, commissioner

ILLUSTRATOR
*Jeanie Leach*

9

# 3

## You Got To Move It, Move It

———◦———

ALL TEN PIECES IN THESE TALES RELATE IN ONE WAY OR another to the theme of motion — *movement*. These songs push, scratch, swirl, glide, slink, groove, and whiz. They dance — they waltz, swing, strut, and sashay. There was a conscious focus on making the language of this music speak in verbs and adverbs. But these songs also dream out loud, often in twelve-bar rhythm and blues, subdivided into two-bar phrases that pile up in a relatively even and straightforward manner, balanced in architectural chunks of four, eight, twelve, and sixteen.

Still, a charted blueprint fails to capture the musical essence of St. Augustine's "subtracto fundamento in aere aedificare" — "build on air without foundation" — those metaphorical castles in the sky. How exactly does one venture beyond the structural parameters to play in metaphysical territory, to suggest the infinite?

What can I tell you?

*Caricature Portrait, November 2011, by Anthony Jenkins*

I'm a storyteller.

As tales tend to do, they offer obvious revelations about the source.

Blossoming from the hints offered by small riffs and licks, the process of composition then underwent the due diligence of organic growth, customary in my music making. Eventually, larger musical narratives evolved, building upon the intimations.

And all the tales have something else in common — they're about the electric guitar that has been at the root of so much historical music making — the Telecaster.

*"subtracto fundamento in aere aedificare"*

# 4

# TELECASTER — IN PURSUIT OF THE TRUTH

———◆———

WHAT'S IN A NAME?
In 1950, Fender introduced their first version of an electric guitar with its own unique shape and features, called a Broadcaster. When Gretsch started making unhappy noises about the infringement on their already-established brand name, Fender responded by snipping the Broadcaster name from the headstock decals that identified the product. (Thus, the guitars made during that 1950 period became known as "No-Casters.") By 1951, referencing the advent of the television era, Fender decided to rechristen the model Telecaster.

Born just two years before your storyteller, the instrument's design has stood the test of time. Rooted in that post–Second World War infatuation with new technologies and the wonders of energy waves beaming through space, folks like Leo Fender were seduced by the power of amplifying signals far and wide, cutting through the noise, both old and new.

Back in the early '50s, country hotshot Jimmy Bryant inspired many imitators, especially with his white Telly glowing on a black-and-white TV. Don Randall, Fender's president of sales, aggressively tried to get Telecasters into the hands of prominent guitarists. By 1958, James Burton had scored a major hit with his Telly on Dale Hawkins's "Susie Q" and appeared on television in Ricky Nelson's band in the hit series *The Adventures of Ozzie and Harriet.* By then, the pedigree was securely established. (I was in kindergarten, blissfully unaware of such developments.)

The baby boom of that postwar period was an expression of hope, potential, and ambition. Perhaps no single invention or creation represents it perfectly, but after The Beatles performed on *The Ed Sullivan Show* on February 9, 1964, nothing on the planet mattered more to me growing up than the electric guitar. And of the hundreds of designs that were flooding the market resonating with the baby boom, the three most iconic to me became the Gibson ES-335, Les Paul, and the Fender Telecaster.

In Toronto's West End, my neck of the woods, used Les Pauls and 335s were so rare as to be mythological, but used Tellies were a bit more accessible and far less expensive. They also seemed more adaptable — in my hometown, *storied.*

If you doubt that, just google Bob Dylan with Robbie Robertson and The Band playing in Manchester, England, in 1966, absorbing the catcall of "Judas" as they tuned up on their Tellies. Before that, Robertson had played in the fabled Yonge Street bars in Rompin' Ronnie Hawkins's band and influenced a young Domenic "Donnie" Troiano, who blazed his way through bands like The Rogues, Mandala, Bush, James Gang, and The Guess Who with his own legendary Telly, with its groundbreaking hot-rod modifications, along for the ride. Troiano even gave that guitar a nickname — Cinderella.

Undoubtedly, an influence on both Robertson and Troiano would have been Steve Cropper, guitarist in the Stax Records house band, Booker T. and the M.G.'s, and producer of many hit records in the '60s down in Memphis, Tennessee. In my little corner of the world, I was coming of age and finally growing aware of Cropper's Telecaster work in 1965 and '66 on "Green Onions," "Knock on Wood," "Soul Man," and "Hold On I'm Coming."

All this inspiration motivated many fledgling Toronto-area guitarists to save up and buy their own Tellies.

Which is exactly what I did. As high school was winding down, my journey as a professional musician began with a second-hand, cream-finish, maple-fingerboard Telecaster, purchased in 1971 from the Long & McQuade music store near Yonge and Bloor Streets in Toronto for 250 bucks. I can't recall if I gave it a nickname; in all likelihood, my own poetic chutzpah hadn't fully kicked in yet.

But I can say this: I often fell asleep with it. A storyteller had begun a life journey with his Telecaster — his Excalibur, his wizard wand, divining rod, security blanket, talking stick, jester's marotte, passport to the universe — this year's, this season's, this week's holy grail — the translation tool of baby-boomer metaphor and allusion.

I'd bought into the Telecaster culture's bloodline.

The boundaries of my teenage education expanded from Robertson and Troiano, leading me beyond the Telly licks of Dora, Missouri's Steve Cropper to the London, England-based stints of Yardbirds Eric Clapton, then Jeff Beck, as well as Jimmy Page (all on Tellies); the aforementioned Roy Buchanan from Ozark, Arkansas; Jimmy Bryant from Moultrie, Georgia; and James Burton from Webster Parish, Louisiana. Telecasters were go-to guitars for both The Funk Brothers in Detroit's Motown and The Wrecking Crew in the studios of Los Angeles. Some of these influences came to me from the radio. Other sources were the record collections of musical friends who were a bit older and hipper than me.

Roy Buchanan became my most important early Telly influencer. "The Messiah Will Come Again" (1972) seemed to have an epic combination of style, chops, character, and tone. A profound integrity seemed to exist between the player, the guitar, the amplifier, and the music on offer. This was something that *demanded* emulation.

Yet, here's an indisputable reality of the Telecaster. A few years later, an even stronger strain of my romantic obsession with the model was sown by the warm, rounded, exquisite tone of Ed Bickert, widely considered the most eloquent of all Canadian jazz guitarists. His instrument of choice was a heavily worn — but demonstrably expressive, perfectly appropriate — blonde 1965 model with a rosewood fingerboard. Established within the traditional, stylistic demographic that favoured big, beautiful archtop guitars, Bickert and his no-frills instrument possessed the same qualities of modesty and economy that informed his music. Even though they were practically polar musical opposites, so dramatically different in tone, Bickert possessed the same exacting integrity that Buchanan displayed.

One guitar model can cover that gamut?

One guitar . . . to rule them all.

What to call it — Telecaster-itis? A bandwagon? A cult? It's been a part of my life since high school, encompassing dozens of players deserving of mention. Some in particular took the instrument to places I can only dream about, leaving me gobsmacked in wonder and admiration.

All the guitarists I'm name-dropping in this book are one of a kind. But when it comes to Blackguard Telly practitioners, Ted Greene and Danny Gatton invented entire leagues of their own, with each standing as champions on a higher plane where technique marries sophisticated complexities of harmonic knowledge channelled through the guitar fingerboard.

Bill Frisell is another modern proponent of the Telecaster who influenced these tales. In *Bill Frisell, Beautiful Dreamer*, the biography by Philip Watson, Marc Ribot remarked on Frisell's 2003 move to a 1974 model, sharing the following about Frisell's various Telecaster-styled guitars:

> It's hard for a non-guitarist to get the depth of moving to the Telecaster, but it's a huge thing. It's very austere — the least gimmicky and the most direct instrument possible . . . There's no place to hide with a Telecaster . . . It's a technical challenge to do all that amazing stuff that Bill does on a Telecaster . . . that's even more impressive. It's like saying, "Yeah, okay, you can do that — but can you do it on a Telecaster?" And Bill absolutely can. It's also a move to the guitar that is right at the centre of American music. It's the secret language that speaks across the racial divide.

Frisell's style of playing is not very apparent in my original material, but it's the *attitude* that had been influential in the lead-up to making the tales, an attitude that could be embodied in the tone of the guitar. Ribot's eloquent commentary had an immediate potency, nailing the role a Telecaster plays for so many. It hit me like a hurled gauntlet: I had to make my next round of artistic statements happen on a Telecaster.

Julian Lage from Santa Rosa, California, is also expanding upon the Telly jazz tradition of players like Ted Greene and Ed Bickert. In a YouTube interview with the wonderful Rick Beato, Lage speaks about the Telly being the "most honest instrument" that "doesn't hype things terribly." He also said that the Telly had a way of delivering similarities to the "overtones of an acoustic." That really resonated. I'd always felt that, amongst its many characteristics, my Tellies were somehow the most logical, natural, evolutionary, electric step up from how the strings reacted on acoustic guitars. There's a straightforward honesty in the way they set sound waves in motion.

Lage is an endlessly articulate and beautiful player, so it's unsurprising that he's thought the whole Telly thing through and can describe his connectivity to the instrument. On MusicRadar .com, he is quoted as saying, "I'd say the biggest reason why I fell in love with it was just the bluntness of it . . . I like an instrument that . . . doesn't do anything unless you do something. It's a bit masochistic, but it's also quite an education. So, it's a very true instrument, and all Tellies possess that I think."

*Bingo.*

I'm not saying that my Telecastering comes anywhere near Lage's ballpark. I have a more limited, personalized, stylized vocabulary of jazz chops. But it's the attitudinal licence of Lage's and Frisell's adventuring which grants and provokes my obligation to chase solo performances of my own tunes in the Telecaster medium. Some other Telly masters are closer to my bailiwick — Danny Kortchmar and Mike Campbell, for example. In their cases, and with players like Bruce Springsteen and Keith Richards, the Telly works in service to the songs and the rock 'n' roll nature of the licks, within the tones of the recorded tracks.

That's the thing about the Telecaster. Depending on the style of music you're chasing, it can work really well in your pursuit of truth. If you figure out the right part to play and then manage to perform it well, it's a unique storyteller that delivers.

Babs has now become the eighth Telly in the lineage of my guitar collection.

*The medium encompasses and enables a full plate of hard truths.*

# 5

# THE TELL-TALE TELECASTER

## (A POEM)

◂—●—▸

sometimes Babs says
c'mon buddy — get a grip
I know you think about holding me
wonder and worry about how much you care for me

and sometimes you can get really picky
when you're wrestling with your problems
but, eventually, I hope you realize
you're angry and frustrated with yourself
and sometimes you're taking that out on me
until you finally work some things out

that's okay — that's alright. I forgive you

sometimes I talk to Babs
confide in her — take her in hand, cradled on my lap
wrap an arm around her
we work some things out
and others think of it as play
but lots of times she knows that I'm deadly serious
there are plenty of times that she lets me get behind her and hide
and I thank my lucky stars she stands right out in front of me

sometimes, she's there waiting
high-strung but low-key
as if she's asking — so, buddy, what's your story, *this* time?

sometimes she remains neutral as Switzerland
passive — like a mirror

sometimes I sing over her

sometimes — when I feel like she's behaving really well
(or maybe she's simply responding to the gentility of my own conduct)
we resonate together —

sometimes Babs talks to me        shares some secrets
shows me ways of thinking that alone, I'd failed to discover
lays out the difference between truth and lies
leads me up to the limits of my puny humanity
and mocks me for my impatience
my petty smallness        my slow density
I resent her smug objectivity
but that's just me and emotion        in transference again

in the end
she has always
only
been helping to teach me who I am

# 6

# Three Years in the Making

---

IN 2021, I STARTED TO COMPOSE A NEW ROUND OF GUITAR
pieces as we went beyond that year tweaking the guitar's
design. The process stretched deep into 2023, as I got to know
Babs intimately while finishing writing.

With Blair Packham as my engineer, the ten pieces were recorded and edited in eight sessions scattered between November 11 and December 2, 2023. Mixing went down on December 6, 8, and 9, with remixes from January 10 to 18, 2024. Steve Skingley mastered the ten tracks later in January.

Meanwhile, I started writing the first draft of this book from November 2023 into February 2024. (Edits were still going on in September of that year.)

Some stories are character-driven. This collection of ten tales actually features five principal characters: Rik, Babs, and the musical trio of rhythm, melody, and harmony. Oh, there's a supporting cast — an electric guitar requires amplification, a recording requires an engineer, the audio signal gets processed with effects, et cetera. But the tales play out *principally* through the interactions of the five lead actors.

Yes, a solo instrumental guitar album is bare-bones, but I didn't harbour the ambition or feel the need to add a rhythm section, overdubs, or even lyrics. If listeners feel something is missing in the musical tales, well — there's over 35,000 words here trying to explain what these five characters are getting on about.

— • —

There's another story within these stories.

At the tail end of 2023, my wife Jeannette and I flew 6,106 kilometres to Gothenburg, Sweden, to join over 3,500 other Canadians watching a bunch of young men play hockey in the World Junior Championship. I was invited there to entertain a large Canadian contingent in a New Year's Eve concert.

We performed a set of twenty-six songs, which came and went. (Now you hear 'em, now you don't.)

That's one thing that music does. It lives in the moment, and then the moment is gone. (Bring on the next.)

After the gig, hopelessly jet-lagged, I stared out our rainswept hotel bedroom window at the impressive Christmas lights exhibit in the Liseberg amusement park, right across the street from the Gothia Towers where we were staying. The highlight of the display was a shooting star, consisting of as many as fifty strands of digital light bulbs spreading down and out from a star at its pinnacle, with a glowing red ruby at its centre, all suspended from the huge 116-metre-tall AtmosFear drop tower attraction.

It was an incredible sight, but something was even more strikingly beautiful, out there in the dark beyond my window. An image of the display was reflected in full life-size by the mirrored facade of a companion Gothia tower over to my left, as rivers of rain ran down its glass, contributing yet another twinkling, shimmering layer to the impressive spectacle: in effect, doubling up the *wow* factor.

As I stood there gobsmacked, admiring that skyrocketing star and its reflection, I had a small epiphany. I didn't even realize it at first, but the Star of Bethlehem Christmas story was the originating layer in that installation. That artificial, festive LED metaphor, with its reflection in the impressive man-made architecture, was actually superimposed on yet another layer in the story — an image within an image within an image.

*Layers.*

That got me thinking about my ten tales.

There I was at 4:30 a.m. in that rainswept New Year's morning moment — a moment that will stick in my brain until memory fails because all those layers of metaphorical symbols imprinted the extraordinary nature of that experience.

I thought, *music is like that.* As simple as a solitary electric guitar instrumental recording is, the songs of my Ten Telecaster Tales are also very much like shimmering, twinkling reflections of ideas: metaphorical stories that provide an ephemeral, sensual, auditory experience, conjuring emotions, stimulating and provoking thoughts and feelings. Mother Nature superimposes a layer; the passage of time contributes yet another elaboration. Oh-so-human intellectualizing, sentimentalizing, rationalizing ...

I was standing there, thinking about my parents, myself, my children, and my children's children — how our lives, our stories, our emotions, are like fireworks, stars bursting and burning with glorious beauty. Then they're gone.

Now you see 'em, now you don't.

I thought, *I make music. I tell stories.* They are like mirror reflections where folks can see their own lives and feel their own feelings.

They are their own things, but they're also like ...

- *the famous handprint silhouettes in La Cueva de las Manos, Santa Cruz, Patagonia, Argentina, that date back over 10,000 years;*
- *initials carved into a park bench (KILROY WAS HERE);*
- *tears in the rain swallowed up in rivers that run to the ocean;*
- *genetic mutations, slight alterations in the chromosomes of guitar history, its bloodlines, with their evolutionary imperatives; and*
- *messages sealed in the grooves of a vinyl disc, or stored in the binary codes of digital files.*

We see and hear these things, now. But the people who made them, back in their moments, are long gone.

Amazing what you can conjure in a jet-lagged, sleep-deprived noggin when you're still high from a gig.

⸻ ◆ ⸻

The creation and production layering of the Ten Telecaster Tales eventually concluded, but only so that the next stratum of stories within stories could begin — with readers and listeners.

Finally feeling confident enough to set the tales free, I grant them their own independent lives, separate from my own. For the stories to continue to grow, I am obliged to share the collaborations with the public. And the public will make of them what they will.

⸻ ◆ ⸻

Smitty, Garren, and I — we designed. Then I composed, arranged and performed. Blair, Steve, and I — we recorded, fixed, mixed, and mastered . . . then we *telecast*.

# 7

## Eli's Loft

———◆———

FOR ALMOST ALL MY LIFE, I DID MY WRITING AND RECORDING work in windowless basements or converted commercial warehouses. In 2023, after an extensive house renovation, my workspace for writing, practising, and recording became a dream come true: a glorious 18-by-23-foot elevated second-floor loft with a cathedral ceiling and triple-aspect windows that I call Eli's Loft.

Across its south side, there's a 15-foot-wide open staircase, with three steps down to a library, housing my guitar collection on full display, beside a large stained-glass window surrounded by bookcases on its west wall. (The central image of the stained glass is a highly stylized fleur-de-lys, symbolizing faith, hope, and love, rendered in white, surrounded by purples and blues. Well — whaddayaknow? A stained-glass window with layers of its own stories to tell.)

*My Library Window*

But why is this studio space called "Eli's Loft"?

That's because, about 12 feet high up on the north wall, above the surrounding windows, there's a whole *other* story: a turn-of-the-twentieth-century wooden carousel horse, flying in all his glory, keeping watch over my creative activities.

*Eli The Wonder Horse Takes Flight*

Back in the '80s, I amputated his left front and rear legs, repainted the dipped-and-stripped creature, and put a large Gothic capital E for Emmett on his saddle blanket before installing him on the grand central staircase wall in our old house. Then, after the kids had moved out and we downsized to new digs, he became my new studio spirit animal.

That required an improved backstory.

Taking my cue from his monogram, I liked the idea of calling him "Eli The Wonder Horse," because I dig multiple layers of stories within a story.

I've always enjoyed the Laura Nyro song "Eli's Comin'," a tune that spoke of temptation and trying to avoid what might be impossible — our own very human tendencies to bite into the apple, or maybe go for the shortcut to pleasurable fun and games when we should be more disciplined about our, um, ethics. For Ms. Nyro, Eli was an embodiment of both pleasure and danger at the same time. (Ahh — layers in conflict!)

According to the book of Samuel in the Bible, Eli was a priest and a judge of the ancient Israelites in the city of Shiloh. The name Eli comes from Hebrew, meaning "high" or "elevated" — "of God."

In 2 Kings 2, Elijah is a prophet who gets carried straight up into heaven by a chariot of fire.

(A chariot needs a horse, right?)

This leads us off on a tangent to *Chariots of Fire*, a film about achievement through self-sacrifice and moral courage. The phrase "chariots of fire" originated in the Bible (2 Kings 6:17). The film's title was inspired by a line from the William Blake poem "And Did Those Feet in Ancient Time":

*Bring me my Bow of burning gold:*
*Bring me my arrows of desire:*
*Bring me my Spear: O clouds unfold!*
*Bring me my Chariot of fire!*

That poem was adapted into the British hymn and (unofficial) English anthem, "Jerusalem," heard at the end of the film.

Blake has been described as radical and antagonistic, evident by his issues with authority. I can relate to the layers of a conflicted artistic state and his own committed spirituality, which spawned his hostility to the Church of England (and apparently to almost all forms of organized religion).

Highly ironic, then, that Blake's creative poem has been adapted, orchestrated, and fixed as a cultural staple of the British establishment. (I appreciate stories that have a layer of irony in them.)

His childhood featured mystical religious experiences — episodes where he thought he'd seen God's face pressed against his window, or witnessed angels among the haystacks. At one point, he believed he'd had a visit from the Old Testament prophet Ezekiel. I wonder if these incidents of a supernatural kind might have been sparked by hyperreligiosity in his frontal and temporal lobes, as well as the limbic system of his brain. (Many contemporaries thought him quite mad.) Nevertheless — I remain somewhat sympathetic to the power of Blake's belief in his own imagination, which led him to his life's work as an artist and poet. Influenced by the ideals and ambitions of the French and American revolutions, something within him was always seeking the divine, beyond the surface realities of the physical world. I can relate to psychological struggles in the balancing act between humanity and spirituality and respect the conflict between the body and our vivid intellectual imagination.

In *The Marriage of Heaven and Hell*, Blake tries to rationalize and balance virtue and vice, the sacred and the profane — a common theme in the creation of a great deal of art. Some of that layering can be heard in my work — even in the purely instrumental noodlings in the tales . . . The recording of which brings us back to Eli's Loft.

As I ponder creative ideas and wonder what choice I should make, I like to imagine that my carousel horse is a benign, inanimate, yet poetic authority figure, reminding me that my attention-deficit distractions of wonder should become more goal-oriented.

I like metaphors. I like lofty ideas that turn into creative work — songs and stories . . . tales of wonder.

I like that my workspace is an over-the-top luxury version of an artist's garret. In a way — similar to the poetic Telly licence that other 'caster masters flaunt — Eli's Loft contributed to my new (and renewed) sense of freedom, providing the courage to write enough tunes to take yet another kick at the recording can.

I also like that my elevated, high-flying carousel horse gazes down upon my world of wondrous proceedings and warns me:

> Eli's not coming, dude.
> He's right here. *Always.*
> And he's not going anywhere.
> So get back to work, brother.
> Make the *right* kind of choices.

# 8

# Background and Foreground

---•---

My last active touring dates were back in January 2019. I notified my agents that I would no longer consider offers for concert appearances. I stopped paying union dues and applying for work visas. Then in March 2020, COVID arose, bringing with it the anxiety and insecurity of a world in lockdown.

Along with that came a bonanza for work-from-home and introspective cocooning. Our beleaguered medical systems experienced a secondary consequence, an epidemic of mental health issues. This exacerbated a world divided into selfish polarities in the era of fake and faker news on social media. Conspiracy theorists abounded in the burgeoning digitization of our universe.

Isolation and disenfranchising led everyone toward more soul-searching. For some, it made them belligerent about wanting the world to reflect their own beliefs regarding cultural values, and they wanted the power to impose that on society. It got ugly, and as far as I can tell, that siloing of divisive attitudes has only grown more intense.

This regrettable social/cultural warfare has reinforced my liberality — my belief in creative freedom, human imagination and ingenuity, and the unfettered importance of stories. It solidified my own self-realizations about what the creative process meant to me and my mental health — how it offered purpose and fulfillment.

Art, music, poems, and stories sparked the reinvention of my life in the months leading up to the release of my first book of poetry in September 2021, logically and unsurprisingly entitled *Reinvention*. If six decades of songwriting had not done a good enough job, shifting my creative focus to poetry reinforced some valuable lessons in the following dynamics: condensing, distilling, packing, and unpacking.

All of that soul-searching stood me in good stead for the two years honing my memoir, *Lay It On The Line*. Analyzing the perspective of a lifetime and editing it down to less than 300 pages was a lengthy exercise in self-awareness. Always a person of multi-hyphenated interests, this jack of many trades preferred stylistic fusion that defied categories, always looking to build metaphorical bridges as opposed to fortress walls.

Self-styled, self-taught, small *r* "renaissance" tendencies reinforced certain truisms about my creativity. I'm big on layers of narrative. As René Descartes philosophized, "cogito, ergo sum" — "I think, therefore I am."

And I know that I like to write.

# Dear Diary

A memoir is a life story, and the subsequent promotion cycle for the book brought full realization of its surreality. It was as if I was invited to my own funeral wake — so much talking about myself in the past tense. But like a character from Monty Python's *Holy Grail*, I wasn't dead yet. So, I began asking myself — where will I go from here? What might await the third act of my life? How might I combine my particular set of mental and physical skills in a personal and unique way (as I head gently — hopefully slowly, nevertheless, surely — with graceful dignity into that good night)?

In the past, playing guitar had always been the central focus of my foreground activity. Since my retirement from the road and the arrival of COVID, creative writing moved centre stage, relegating the guitar to the background. I've always been an inventive type, but since my childhood, I've also been a guitarist.

Nevertheless, after my sixty-fourth birthday I'd drifted away from the gravitational pull of the guitar. Four and a half years later, the time felt overdue to return to six strings, all kinds of chords, and the Truth. I also loved the idea that the guitar could once again speak for me, and I wouldn't have to natter about myself. (Doing rounds of promotion gets you mighty sick of your own voice.)

Of course — there's an obvious irony in the fact that I default to the guitar, in order to express myself, without talking about myself; then write music that is in large part, autobiographical; and then proceed to write a book that is in large part, *me*, talking about me.

*Oh my.*

Well — the strength of the guitar's gravitational pull on me may not be consistent, but it's constantly present. It waxes and wanes, but by 2022, its voice was calling again, as loudly as it ever had. As I've done all my life, I responded.

As already established, the Telecaster is a celebrated vehicle for searching out truth. It facilitates *honesty* with autobiographical *authenticity* and *integrity*. These buzzwords of our times generate plenty of problematic rubs.

Starting back in the 1990s, and for the next few decades, I'd served on advisory boards, done committee work, and been involved in situations where many ethical terms — accountability, transparency, authenticity, integrity, credibility — were bandied about. But I've always had a skeptical relationship with authority — even my own. Despite best intentions and due diligence, I've found that cultural buzzwords can also serve as camouflage, while the real work of truly honouring the dynamics of putting those words into action remains difficult.

That problematic rub can turn into a chafe, and you can get burned.

Certain political factions had arisen and were making noises using these very buzzwords. And there I was, a privileged, wealthy, old white male, in a woke world of cancel culture where hypocrisies are multi-layered. And as the digital universe facilitates the power to generate the spin cycles of marketing, publicity, and promotion, our modernity becomes awash in a relentless onslaught of Orwellian doublethink and double-talk.

The plan for my own creative journey began forming: solo music, no lyrics, no band tracks, no overdubs. Electric guitar — because aging hands and fingers weren't feeling up to the physical challenges of daily workouts on the heavier tensions of acoustic string gauges.

No rhetoric. Get naked and try to stay that way. Write what you know and what you can attempt to play, straight off the floor. Use the brutal honesty of the Telly to find yourself, then just *be* yourself.

However, in June 2023, a new problem struck quite suddenly: polymyalgia rheumatica. This forerunner of rheumatoid arthritis created annoying, inconvenient health battles to wage on two fronts because there was also an unhappy development in my relatively benign slow-growth prostate cancer, which required testing, then more testing, and then a round of radiation therapy in January 2024.

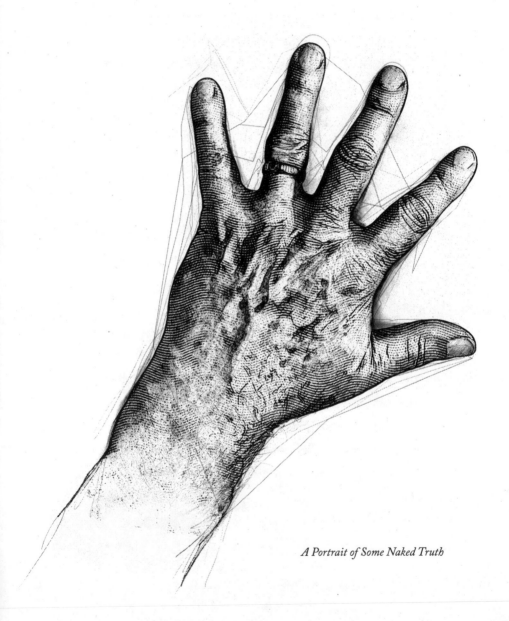

*A Portrait of Some Naked Truth*

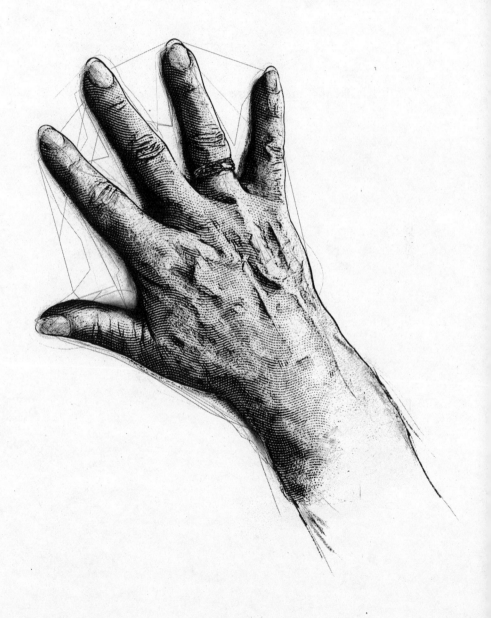

Inconvenient. Frustrating.

All this made me increasingly aware of the ticking of my biological clock — a closing window of opportunity to try and challenge myself as a guitarist, pushing the boundaries of my own technique and creative abilities.

———•——

It felt like the time was now — or maybe never.

# 9

# PERSPECTIVES ON THE GUITAR — DEFYING THE ODDS

---◆---

THE GUITAR IS A SYMBOLIC TALISMAN, A TOOL FACILITATING the delivery of ideas and emotions. But it's also a demanding, complicated instrument with infinite potential. Reflecting the player's personality, it serves as a trusty vehicle for autobiography. But it also allows and encourages performers to display their virtuosity.

Or their politics.

Famously, Woody Guthrie decorated his guitar with the slogan, "This machine kills fascists." His way of thinking inspired many others to rethink their own instrument's raison d'être. Pete Seeger was a bit more of a long-winded peacenik hippie. His banjo's slogan read, "This machine surrounds hate and forces it to surrender." Guitarist Tom Morello of Rage Against the Machine, Audioslave, and others — including a stint in Bruce Springsteen's touring E Street Band — was inspired by Guthrie to sloganize many of his electric guitars with phrases like, "Arm the Homeless," "Soul Power," and "Sendero Luminoso" (Shining Path). He's also got an acoustic with the sharpie message, "Whatever It Takes."

Throughout my professional career, politics in my music was always based on a liberal sort of humanism. The bands I was in, the styles of the music I played — likely even the way that I looked, dressed, and cut my hair — never seemed to convey much of my genuine rationalism to third parties. Critical judgments often *superficially* reported that I was (for better or worse) trying to *superficially* impress with my guitar technique and prowess. I certainly don't deny that I tried to make the best of my skill set, but I can't accept that I was merely a show-off making one-dimensional *superficial* music.

This remains a bit of a double whammy for me in the Ten Telecaster Tales. My natural tendencies lead to a fair amount of guitar virtuosity, and some of that stuff informs the tales. But none of this work was ever intended to be pyrotechnical state of the art. It's not false humility to describe the music as tunes or melodies built within accessible song forms. What you hear in the recordings is just me, being me. In particular, I aimed for things that came naturally, that my brain, heart, and hands could almost take for granted. In some instances, *fancy*, sure, but *fun*.

The goal was to be musical — make it sound effortless and smooth. Plus, display a sense of humour from time to time (to time). There's a spectrum, and some depth, but I hoped my joy of playing would animate the proceedings.

There are also some moments of melancholy blue sorrow. All of this was intended to come off as authentic, not contrived or showbiz busy.

The tales are not pop songs but *guitar songs*. Sixty years of experience raises the technical bar some, but I was going for natural guitarisms, springing from long traditions of licks based on chord forms, shapes, and patterns on the fingerboard and the phrasing they facilitate. More of a songwriter than a jazz fingerstyle virtuoso, the pieces are leavened with accessible forms — not fabrications of progressive art.

My guitar playing is also informed by my identity as a singer. There's a wide range of stylistic ways that singers end up playing their guitars. George Benson's pyrotechnical fluidity as a guitar soloist owes a lot to the incredible ad-lib singing he can conjure in his head. Eric Clapton has a very different style, yet his fluid blues phrasing is heavily influenced by his feel for pentatonic melodies singing throughout his entire being. I'm no Benson or Clapton, but there's evidence of my singing style in the way I phrase my guitar compositions. That's just a natural tendency, and I don't fight it — I go with it.

Having said that, I should also quickly acknowledge another thing revealed in my memoir. I'm a one-percenter in the general population, with my cross-dominant brain wired so that fine motor control is right-handed and gross motor control is left-handed. It's my opinion that a disproportionately large number of professional guitarists have some measure of cross-dominance. According to my personal theory, that's what likely leads us to the guitar in the first place, where we discover we like it, and it seems to like us back — so we stick with it. And because of my left-handed gross motor tendencies, I tend to use a lot of ligado, hammer-on, and pull-off techniques in my compositions and performance.

As the seeds of my Telecaster tales sprouted some tender, wee shoots of growth, I tried to develop along the same creative lines and employ the same general process for all of them. What story is the melody starting to tell? A chord progression begins to suggest a setting or a landscape, but it's also generating a ballpark of style, as I listen very intently for the emergence of the rhythm that will make or break the value of the entire creation.

Rhythm is the key. Rhythm rules and regulates. Rhythm is the dynamic generator that needs a heartbeat before I can claim, "It's alive! *It's alive!*"

I also find myself working in the same territory that all commercial songwriters do, hoping that the marriage of a melody atop a chord progression is unique and original. We all want the melody and the chord progression to give off a sense of comfortable familiarity, generating a positive reaction on the very first listen. There are a few centuries of melodies on the books for the diatonic music of the civilized world. For popular music, that's a narrow tightrope to walk because no one wants to get dismissed for being derivative — or worse, sued for plagiarism.

An extremely attractive and familiar creation still requires its own fingerprints and DNA. You have to keep writing, rewriting, and tweaking until it has established its own unique identity.

Here's my favourite analogy regarding the process of creative writing. Tyrus Raymond Cobb remains the most successful hitter in the history of major league baseball. This GOAT's lifetime batting average was .367 — which means he *failed* in his task over 60 percent of the time.

I like to remind creative artists: "That's life."

Compare that to *these* odds: the ejaculate of an average male contains somewhere between 80 to 300 million sperm. At an estimate, a few hundred survive the journey to a viable egg if the stars align with an ovulation cycle. Then, there's maybe a 7 to 10 percent success rate of an egg becoming fertilized.

Somehow or other, we're pushing 8 billion human beings on Planet Earth.

Which is to say — every single little Telecaster seed of mine had a germinating flicker of hope inside it, struggling to catch up and join the human race.

In a way, I like to think of these ten tales as oh-so-human underdogs, defying the odds.

# 10

# ARCHETYPES AND POETIC FAITH

—◄ ● ►—

THE GUITAR CAN BE SEEN AS PRACTICAL — TECHNICAL — mathematical. A series of notes are lettered, scaled, and numbered. Strings and frets, likewise. This builds geometric grids, patterns, and shapes. Once certain techniques have been reliably established, music emerges that can be captured by the ones and zeroes of the digital universe. Those sounds can be converted into conventional, quantifiable markings on a manuscript. An ability to communicate via music's theory and harmony further enhances the practical applications of guitar technique. There are scientific aspects to its arts and crafts; I'm not proud but also not ashamed to admit that's definitely my weakest link. (I believe artists need self-awareness of strengths *and* weaknesses.)

Still — the guitar can also be poetic, metaphorical, romantic, and as infinitely elusive as the creative art that can happen on it. (Now we're talking my language.)

Just how poetic might a guitar become? (I'm glad I asked. *Ahem* . . .)

*My favourite tree in the neighbourhood is an ancient silver maple, likely over 180 years old. The neck and fingerboard on Babs are made of maple. I don't know if this silver maple dreams of reincarnating as a guitar, but the poet in me enjoys the notion.*

"To a Lady, with a Guitar," is a fanciful poem written in 1822 by Percy Bysshe Shelley, accompanying the gift of (duh) a guitar to a friend. In the second stanza of the poem, Shelley dreamed of a tree that died in its sleep, feeling no pain, then went on to live in "happier form again" as, of course, a guitar. Shelley imagined that the guitar's luthier had designed the guitar in such a way that it would reply justly and skillfully to those who questioned it, in its own gentle language. Here's how he describes the nature of that language:

> Whispering in enamoured tone
> Sweet oracles of woods and dells
> And summer winds in sylvan cells:
> For it had learned all harmonies
> Of the plains and of the skies,
> Of the forests and the mountains,
> And the many-voiced fountains;
> The clearest echoes of the hills,
> The softest notes of falling rills,
> The melodies, of birds and bees,
> The murmuring of summer seas,
> And pattering rain, and breathing dew,
> And airs of evening; and it knew
> That seldom-heard mysterious sound,
> Which, driven on its diurnal round,
> As it floats through boundless day,
> Our world enkindles on its way:
> All this it knows, but will not tell
> To those who cannot question well
> The Spirit that inhabits it;
> It talks according to the wit
> Of its companions; and no more
> Is heard than has been felt before,
> By those who tempt it to betray
> These secrets of an elder day:

*But, sweetly as its answers will*
*Flatter hands of perfect skill,*
*It keeps its highest, holiest tone*
*For our beloved friend alone.*

Shelley's poem might have been the solidification of an arche-type — the romantic appeal of a poetic, spiritual communion, an organic and natural union, between the instrument and its player. That notion had likely been around before, and maybe it's only my convenient perception that Shelley provided the world with this poetic tipping point. One thing's certain — those romantic manifestations have never gone out of style.

We humans have our egotistical tendencies to anthropo-morphize and personify. Consider how famous players have named their guitars — Stevie Ray Vaughan's First Wife; B.B. King's Lucille; both George Harrison and Albert King had their own Lucy; Neil Young's Old Black and Clapton's Blackie; Billy Gibbons's Pearly Gates; Willie Nelson's old Trigger; Keith Richards's Micawber . . . Here, in my tales, I have been waxing poetic about Troiano's and Bickert's Tellies — and my own, the seductive, inviting, mercurial, and eclectic Babs.

Generating backstory remains a fairly popular pursuit. After all, many of us are searching for clues — trying to drop hints.

———◆▸———

My own detective work led me to the following basics for poetic storytelling.

In 1817, Samuel Taylor Coleridge described the willing suspension of disbelief as a kind of "poetic faith" that occurs between author and reader. By 1939, J.R.R. Tolkien defined and upgraded the paradigm to one of "secondary belief" wherein an author is obliged to generate a creative world and atmosphere that allows his reader/audience to find the narrative and events sufficiently truthful. (Call it a reader's "gimme" for the author's due diligence in generating fictional plausibility.)

As I went through the process of composing, rehearsing, and then recording the Telecaster Tales, the overriding elements that I kept trying to measure the work against were instinctive and organic. Only in trying to articulate it for this text did I arrive at, and settle on, the notions of poetic faith and secondary belief. Still — they resonate. The ten tales had to hang together, separate and distinct, yet sharing a metaphysical vibe that could make the overall narrative sound believable. My own technique had to play at a certain level, within a specific musical vocabulary, to satisfy my sense of what appropriately belonged. But in the back of my head, there's also a voice asking me if the average listener out there is going to buy in, or at least give me the benefit of the doubt.

Another ongoing creative challenge is to provide insights and perspectives on the metaphysics of layering — how the stories within the stories within the story relate and integrate.

In the end, a tune plays. A listener is not obligated to seek out, know, or understand anything at all about the layers. The only thing that matters is that, hopefully, they can experience an emotional connection to what they're hearing. Does the auditory experience work? Can they feel the truth resonate?

As with any of my creative endeavours, the musical tales provide yet another example of me trying to find myself. Beyond that, I now find myself here at my writing desk, explaining how I went about creating the potential for that tintinnabulation to make sense to listeners — to take the vague outlines of a story and imbue it with music, then build the music along with the story, and tell those stories in the language of solo guitar pieces.

How can I get the average listener to willingly suspend their disbelief, find it sufficiently truthful, and enter into a mutual understanding about the songs based on poetic faith?

That's a two-step process. First, that connection relies on mental, physical, emotional, and spiritual cues making themselves apparent in the music itself — that's my job as a writer. Then a communion must be made manifest through my performance as an artist before it can ever translate to a listener.

Two steps toward communion: but it will be in vain if those steps fail to generate poetic faith and secondary belief in the hearts and minds of an audience.

# 11

# OUTSIDE IN, INSIDE OUT

———◂●▸———

HE SPIRITUAL COMMUNION OF AN INSTRUMENT AND human being also requires connectivity and bonding between the Head, Hands, and Heart — the triangulated three *H*'s of the mental (what happens inside) that leads to the physical (outside). The brain connects to the hands and fingers, which need to be informed not just by the intellect of the brain but also by the emotion that is appropriate to the music that the ears are hearing.

These dynamics are the lifeblood of the creative spirit. The outside enters in, and the artist absorbs and considers it. Then the three *H*'s combine to work on what's inside and turn themselves (and their work) inside out.

When we speak of certain artists having a rare gift, which elevates their work and separates them from the pack, we are acknowledging that they seem to have an incredible, seamless flow between the physical, intellectual, and emotional. (I'll dig deeper into this particular eternal triangulation later on.)

It's not something that can always be taken for granted. For example, a very real affliction of musicians who wear out the neural connectivity to their physical skills is called *focal dystonia* — a neurological condition causing involuntary muscle contractions that affect the hands, wrists, or arms, which can affect the fine motor skills of musicians, athletes, surgeons, dentists, calligraphists, and hairstylists.

But when everything is working in a miraculous way — when it can be completely taken for granted, like an autonomic function — it is a glorious and wondrous thing. Music teachers, tutors, and mentors keep trying to get their students to discover and focus on the development of their voice. Certainly, a part of that is their own unique character and personality — whatever is inside them *connects* the physical, mental, and emotional elements of creativity. But surely, it's also that flow of idea, instinct, and emotion translating into physicality.

A singer's voice is monophonic, just as brass and woodwind instruments are — which is to say, they can only produce one note at a time. But an additional layer for guitarists is that our instrument can be polyphonic, producing as many as six notes at once. (More, if we start counting harmonic overtones.)

The piano keyboard is the obvious champion of this game — eighty-eight keys laid out — and by holding down the sustain pedal on the floor, you can get as many of those notes ringing out as you'd like. But piano notes originate from hammers hitting strings: they're mechanical. Whereas a fingerstyle guitarist has the skin, muscle, nail, and bone of up to ten fingers conjuring notes directly from the strings. The voice that a guitarist develops has a wider range than a human voice, with its potential for up to six voices of polyphonic harmony. This expanded voice — internalized, then externally produced — can generate an obsessive fascination. There's an infinite potential for variations of touch to sound, and of melody to harmony. Married to the spiritual, physical, mental, and emotional potential that can be embodied in one note, one phrase, one passage, there's little wonder why the guitar has possessed and projected so much romantic imagination for so long.

———•———

Given the right playing, the guitar turns us all *inside out*.

*Guitarist Inside Outside Principle*

# 12

# MY WHEELHOUSE
# AND MY WOODSHED

◆ ● ▶

WITH RESPECT TO THE RECORDINGS OF THESE TEN compositions, and the kinetic dynamics between my physical, mental, emotional, and spiritual characteristics, here's my confession on self-perception.

Naturally, every listener is free to develop their own subjective interpretation of what they're hearing, how it speaks to them, and in what proportions. But I have a personal take on my strengths and weaknesses — qualities as well as challenges.

I established two ground rules for myself as I began composing the pieces. I didn't want to write above my own head, and I wanted to try and keep the material within my own (technical, physical) wheelhouse, as it were.

(Tangent: you *can* write above your own head, in terms of performance skills. The digital technology of computer recording and infinite manipulation of sound files makes almost any figment of imagination possible. You can easily create a recorded version of a song, then worry about whether or not you might actually be able to execute a live performance of it *later*.)

This governing of my creativity went hand in hand with another strong (and recurring) self-realization: I didn't invent any of the wheels in my wheelhouse. I'm not a technical innovator or a theoretical pioneer looking to break moulds. I'm a traditionalist, simply drawn to some "wheels" that speak to me. Then I come to terms with how I can get the notes I hear inside my head to emerge from the strings of the instrument. Whenever I resort to off-the-beaten-path things like — oh, using my left thumb for fretting a bass note, or employing the proximal phalanx or metacarpal of my index finger to extend the range of my left-hand fingerings — I know that George Van Eps and Tal Farlow (amongst others) explored these techniques long before I was even born. I've been lucky enough to witness Lenny Breau perform unfathomable technical wizardry on a guitar, and I had a college teacher, Peter Harris, who developed his own evolution of the Breau approach.

That ain't me.

Still — I do have a personal wheelhouse. And when you hear me playing a piece like "Slinky," I'm pretty comfortable working that musical territory. "Funky Scratchin'" is also a stylistic ballpark that suits me right down to the balls of my tootsies. Whereas "Gee Whiz" and "So Pushy" embody a bit more of a challenge, as the groove starts to require a bit more swing, with jazz sensibilities that apply some pressure on an old bluesy folk-rocker.

I'm halfway to the woodshed with the tracks "Cowboy and Gaucho Waltz" and "Swirling (Courante)." I have to concentrate on keeping those waltzes feeling consistent, and I struggle with adjusting my dynamics so that the recording audio remains within quality parameters. I can get carried away too easily, using my right-hand fingernails to flail away on the strings, beating 'em up, which in turn overloads certain frequencies, generating noisy artifacts that the microphone captures. This moves the challenge of the process up the food chain to the recording and mastering engineers, which I regret. This audio challenge of hyperdynamic EQ arising from the Spanish flamenco / rasgueado style of strumming happened a little in "Burlytown" as well. That playing style comes natural to me, but I'm pretty damn good at slopping paint well outside the lines.

Some stuff requires discipline — a quality I often lack. Compounding this, in certain moments, the emotion I'm putting in motion is my more immediate concern, which makes me careless. I'll deal with the fallout later, leading to the old recording saying, "We'll fix it in the mix," when it could, and likely *should* have been resolved in pre-production rehearsal.

By the time I get to the subtler tracks — "The Rio Glide" and the ballads, "Allemande" and "Winter Nocturne" — I have to fully commit to quality time in the woodshed, where I must relearn lessons about control, restraint, and the emotional power of letting notes speak in eloquent phrases before I rush ahead to more and more notes. In ballads, the autobiographer of "So Pushy" has to go against his instincts, applying himself intellectually, harnessing some physical and emotional performance tendencies into the service of other artistic dimensions.

The softer, gentler ballad tracks were my greatest challenges within the tales. The valley of shadows has always been my deepest, toughest artistic no man's land. The emotional toll of sorrow and melancholy — the restraint that informs the character of softer pieces — generates some aversion. I want to go there, but I also don't want to have to remain at work there for too long.

Nevertheless, sadness is an inescapable reality of our existence, and a calm, measured consideration of it is a reasonable response. That dimension needs to make its presence felt, somewhere in a collection of music that I create, in order for me to consider the work artistically balanced and complete.

One more transparent admission should be made here, since I've alluded to writing above my own head and wanting to be able to play everything live off the floor.

That's not the way it worked out.

But we'll delve into the saving graces of digital editing shortly.

*Wheelhouses In The Woodshed*

# 13

## Layers

———◆———

*Triangulations*

THIS BOOK DISSECTS AND ANALYZES THE LAYERED CAKE
that was a recording project of ten electric guitar instrumental pieces. One layer is literally and obviously *literary*, with
solar flares shooting off into the poetic. That imaginative layer

can expand to universal proportions — the infinite layer — or contract to sub-atomic particles, where the germs of never-ending self-doubt breed.

Guitar playing is always a three-way marriage between emotional, physical, and intellectual layers. Bypassing the emotional component for now, let's examine the intellectual and the physical perspectives in depth, allowing emotional aspects to arise more naturally later on in the analysis.

Intellectually, the first thought of designing a guitar gave birth to strategic planning, organizing a musical territory to explore, followed by creating and composing several stories comprised of melody, harmony, and rhythm. The composer's intellect plays within their own limitations of understanding the relationship of notes to each other — in scales, within chords — and the creative development of stories (tales) that are making their own kind of conceptual and structural sense.

All this mental architecture then has to shift over and get located on a guitar fingerboard. Voicings? Positions? Fingerings? The mind *boggles*, leading to the mental gymnastics of envisioning that fretboard, calculating distances, and organizing the dynamics of touch. Brain computations precede bodily mechanics, determining the complexities of interaction between the body parts connecting with the guitar itself, eventually generating the sound waves that the brain has been conjuring.

But before it gets to be music, flying through the air with the greatest of ease, there are very real, physical challenges — the laying on of hands, playing the guitar. Seems simple enough — and appears so, when good players make it happen with such cool, easy style. But this may be the most complex layer of all because so much of it relies on the senses. Three of the basic five senses are being coordinated — hearing, sight, and touch.

During the extended pre-production period for the Telecaster Tales, I became obsessed with a particular quality of Ed Bickert, checking out his videos on YouTube: he was able to play extended, complicated sections of music *with his eyes closed*. (Instagram clips confirm that dozens of players I've never even heard of before can do this kind of thing, too.) Whenever I attempt too much blind physicality, the results of position shifts for fingerings leave much to be desired.

The synergy between Bickert's brain and hands functioned on a deeper level than I can manage. I need my eyes to help me out — to lead the way, in certain situations. Another way to look at this is — Bickert could move from one layer to another (the mental to the physical) without engaging the layer of his sense of sight in between. I can do this a bit, but not a lot. I usually need that extra layer.

This taught me something. Kevin Costner has said that if you don't understand your limitations, you won't achieve much in your life. Challenges in skill sets means facing up to limitations. Music making must entertain the bandwidths of capacity — dimensions and proportions you might not even possess in the first place. And what *is* there might not find its way to the hands easily and fluidly because one's sensory layers slow down the process.

Well, Mr. Costner — I do want to achieve something. Insight into my own process led to certain measures of resolve for pursuing my own Telecaster Tales. My layering is certainly different than that of many accomplished jazz guitarists.

The challenge: make my layering work well for me.

This realization quickly led to others. I stopped entertaining the notion of heavier-gauge flatwound strings that a jazzer might have used. As a "rock" kind of guy (coping with the growing challenge of arthritis), the light top–heavy bottom string tension I was accustomed to suited me. Plus — as a singer by trade, my own writing and arranging could and should lean toward what I heard singing in my head, as opposed to what might be characterized as the intellectualizing of musical vocabulary that could come pouring out (so intimidatingly) through others' hands.

Additionally, my rock 'n' roll roots influence me to employ what I think of as guitar punctuation and vocal stylings. String glissandos and ghosted notes are included for rhythmic effect. Thumps on the strings; bent notes; wide, generous vibrato; slurs — messy kinds of grace-note slide-ins and tail-offs. I allowed myself to get a bit greasier: down and dirtier. (Blair and I accepted some stuff because it was "guitary.")

Yeah, I have bumps and bruises on my big fat head from the school of hard knocks. I need my eyeballs to scout out some landing locations. Very well — these are characteristics of my tales.

Additionally, I realized that my lifetime of playing led me to employ my emotions a fair bit in my process. In particular, this aforementioned element of greasy, guitary punctuation seemed to come from an emotional engagement with the material at hand. (But before we go spinning off into a discussion of emotional complications, let's finish with the physical/technical stuff in *this* chapter.)

Obviously, the guitar itself presents yet another physical layer, as it's the hardware setting sound waves in motion. All guitarists get their instruments set up to facilitate their personal technical approach, and I'm no different. I like my string action higher than your average player because I have my cross-dominant brain thing happening and I like the strings to fight back a bit more against my strong left hand. I like the action set up high because I have a weird little habit of using my left-hand pinky to bend the first and second strings a full tone up *underneath* the adjacent strings (as most players push bent strings in and up *against* adjacent strings). I also like the tone of the guitar better with higher action. To my ears, it gives bigger, rounder notes and allows for a bigger range of attack. I can pick harder, and vibrating strings don't buzz or crap out against the frets as much.

Another layer of physicality extended to my playing seated for all the recording sessions, with the guitar on my right thigh, and my right foot perched up on a classical guitar footrest. I tried playing standing up, with a strap across my shoulder, in order to engage my body more fully. After all, I used to earn my living running around on big stages in sports stadiums. But I found I could centre and focus the music better when seated. Tommy Emmanuel is one of my favourite guitarists on the planet. Like a drummer, his whole body is always fully engaged, standing or seated. Granted — as a vocalist, I've always maintained that the making of music benefits from a holistic approach, coming from the soles of your feet right up to the follicles of your scalp. Likewise, as a guitarist, the notes don't just come from your hands or the strings of your instrument. You have to find the best way to get your entire body engaged in generating every note. I still stand up on some recording sessions, when I'm improvising higher-energy rock solos. But for these tales? I wasn't singing, and I needed to be solidly rooted. That was the only way I could cook the recipe.

<hr />

Every layer has to come together to bake the cake properly.

# 14

# The Tightrope Walker's Search for Balance

## ("Both Sides Now")

———◆●▶———

*Standing on a tightrope*
*Suspended above a song*
*Balance on a thin lifeline*
*Defying gravities of right and wrong*
*Searching for the chord that ties it all together*
*For the sake of love forever and ever*
*Stand — and deliver.*

— RIK EMMETT, "STAND AND DELIVER," *Absolutely* ALBUM (1990)

THESE TALES ABOUT THE TALES REVEAL INSTINCTS within my creative process as a writer, performer, and recording artist, where I'm striving to hear what the work is trying to tell me it wants to become. Somehow, I don't feel like I've completed the process until the composition has achieved its own equilibrium.

I've made many references herein to my search for balance. Consider Joni Mitchell's song "Both Sides Now," a creation of wisdom and genius from a person of twenty-three with an influence that will continue across generations of songwriters. In it, the lyric progresses verse by verse, from the metaphor of clouds, to love, and finally to a universal big picture of life itself, with the perspectives from both sides only leading to the singer / writer's understanding of their illusions, and a conclusion that she doesn't really know anything at all. Overflowing with the truth of humanity and the emotions related to our finite existence, a great miracle of this song lies in its own shape, execution, and balance. All its parts make perfect sense in relation to each other: the song grows, and pays off, balanced within the entirety of its conception and execution.

This balancing act is one of the challenges facing any creative artist. Certainly, the architecture of form is of the essence, but that's hardly the whole story. The craft of the business at hand is crucial, and yet "the whole truth and nothing but" rests on what only the artist can feel — an organic instinct that lets you know that the work has achieved its own balance and has come to its own conclusion. Anything taken away would lessen it; anything added would be extraneous. And I deliberately chose to exemplify "Both Sides Now" because its very subject matter is also what I'm going on about here. Granted, I'm suggesting that process is a bit more like "*All* Sides," and not just two. Still — in creative writing (and especially the more accessible constructions of musical creativity), it's easier and cleaner to illustrate a point via the contrast of a duality than to get bogged down in a rainbow spectrum of perspectives.

Going off on a worthwhile tangent here: Leonard Bernstein discussed duality in a television broadcast from his Ford Foundation hour *Omnibus* series in 1954. Bernstein's biographer, Meryle Secrest, captured what he had to say about rhythm in her book *Leonard Bernstein: A Life*.

> *Most music, he pointed out, was based on a dual concept, one that seemed intrinsic to the human condition, just as a heart expanded and contracted.* "We live in a world of up and down back and forth, day and night. In order to exhale we must inhale; there is no third step in the process, no intermediate function. It is in-and-out, in-and-out, 1-2, 1-2." *In imitation of life music was invariably structured with two beats to the bar or multiples thereof. Even bars tended to run in pairs, the first set of notes needing the second in order to complete its musical intentions. Or perhaps it might be a four-bar phrase, or an eight or even a sixteen. As he was quick to concede, the one exception was the triple beat, a theoretical concept and therefore linked to mystical thought, e.g. the Holy Trinity. Nevertheless, however complex most rhythms became, the ultimate building blocks could always be traced to the interaction of two plus two or three plus three and symmetrical combinations thereof, at least to the end of the nineteenth century.*

This ongoing search for the equilibrium of the playground teeter-totter extends to many facets of the creative process. Another one of them (for me, anyway) is balancing an audience's wants and needs with my own artistic self-indulgences. The melodies I write need to possess accessibility and memorability so that even a casual listener might be attracted to what's going on. At the same time, the tunes need to satisfy my own artistic sense of originality, with an element of novelty or surprise in them, so that they feel fresh to me. It's also true that, at the age of seventy, I've written hundreds of songs and there are tendencies and preferential stylizations that might lead some to say, "Oh, that's *really so* you, Rik." I wouldn't want to perversely reject that reality, either. In a sense, that familiarity factor is a strong ingredient in balancing out an audience's desire for accessibility with my own ambition to generate something uniquely new. I can put that to use and happily (or sometimes a bit more grudgingly) meet those folks halfway, as it were.

Apparently, by the time one gets past seventy, strong scavenging and survival instincts have developed.

The guitar community itself is yet another faction of the general public that enters into the dynamics of balancing my wants and needs with those of others. There's a peer group of musicians who read guitar posts on their news feeds, teach guitar, and always look out for the next big thing — the new kid in town. This segment of the demographic market seeks varying measures of physical dexterity, technique, and clever displays of musicianship. They're not usually satisfied for long by pop music's simple accessibility and memorability. They want the music to bristle (at least a bit) with intellectual and physical challenges. They enjoy the privileged feeling of their own connoisseur-club membership. I understand this dynamic well. After all, I was a guitar magazine columnist from '83 to '96, with a professional guitarist's life full of folks who were stage techs, or who worked in music stores: luthiers who built and repaired instruments, and a network of endorsement companies retailing gear. With a creative pallet of instrumental electric guitar fingerstyle pieces, it wouldn't make sense to disregard my peer group in The Guitar Universe. But a niche is also a narrow target, and . . . what if you miss the currency and novelty of its razor-thin cutting edge?

Still — the creative life is an ongoing, never-ending *process*. I'm continuously trying to trust in that process, relying on an instinct for truth and balancing work with my own internal dynamics. The process requires an open heart and mind, which can leave one feeling a bit vulnerable. I've had a lifetime of it, to one degree or another. The question at hand is, what has all that taught me in terms of what I bring to *this* particular offering?

My artistic instinct for the tales was to try and remain a humble seeker — a pilgrim. I sought new ways to my own truth — but a large part of my truth needed to come from a combination of what makes me feel emotionally, intellectually, and physically comfortable, married to candid honesty. I was seeking a better, stronger marriage between those internal elements. As a seeker, perhaps the easiest way to articulate the process is through questions looking for answers — yet another form of *duality*.

Am I advancing my inner and outer self by continuing to make music? At the age of seventy, am I still developing the personal character of my voice? Is my composing more me? More natural? Does the work contain less artifice? Is it less self-conscious and more in tune with itself? Does it seem to have more of the wisdom of maturity? Can I hear it in the music? Do I feel it when I play?

Speaking of feel . . . Is there a liquid quality to the emotion? Does it have a logical flow?

The bottom line: are the qualities and values of my skill set still improving, or are they degrading? This became a fundamental challenge in the production of the tales. With arthritis and cancer knocking on the front and back doors of my metaphorical physical house, I had to be honest with myself about what that stuff was doing to the physical performance of my hands — my chops.

That honesty requires context because it's never just a question of a peer group within the present-day guitar community. There's a long and illustrious history here (naming just some of my own preferences) running from Lonnie Johnson and Eddie Lang through Joe Pass, George Van Eps, Ed Bickert, and Ted Greene to current influencers like Bill Frisell and Julian Lage.

I also (always) have to give special mention to Pat Metheny because I think of him as a stand-alone — the most complete guitar artist alive on this planet. (Composer, recording artist, and touring concert performer, over an incredible range of work.)

Quickly, *easily*, I admit I don't even attempt to run with the likes of that pack, and never could. Still, I feel the need to balance out their influence on what I end up doing on my own journey.

Hey, *I gotta be me*. But even though I'm doing my own thing, I also draw inspiration from legitimate sources and show the guitar community that I respect the values of the bloodlines — yet another compelling force in my search for balance in these compositions and recordings.

There's also the inspirational impact of Joni Mitchell's collaboration with engineer Henry Lewy on the album *Hejira*. In terms of sonics, their approach to recording guitars provided a seminal, fundamental cornerstone for what I set out to build into the tales, sonically speaking.

This leads us to yet another layer in the musical storytelling — the record engineering and production.

# 15

## TRYING TO FIND THE RIGHT MIX FOR THE TALES

———◆———

STARTING OUT WITH AN ELECTRIC GUITAR AND A SMALL combo amp wasn't much different than old school jazzers in by-gone days. Or Joni Mitchell with her Roland JC 120 on *Hejira*. I copped a strong measure of inspiration from the Telecastering attitudes of many others as this project started. These role models work mostly bare-handed, with varying degrees of a subtle reverb effect, although Ted Greene occasionally and exceptionally applied a fair bit of *Encino California* spring reverb — sometimes, almost as much as the glorious *Glendora* reverb wash of The Surfaris; other times channelling pedal steel guitars, crying out in *Bakersfield* country.

Still, throughout the process of recording the ten compositions, I approached the pieces as unaffected as I could. Many tracks did have a taste of digital plate reverb coming from the amp itself. Still, I tried to avoid the use of headphones to monitor or "play into" any effects. I wanted to be present in Eli's Loft, not lost too far inside my head. For tracking, my priority was getting my hands to interpret the notes properly. The thinking was that later, in the mixing stage, Blair and I could concentrate on developing effects treatments, with more room for experimentation, and a more comprehensive focus on generating atmosphere — space, depth, width. For recording off the floor, I wanted to focus on my physical and technical performances without the distraction (and perhaps the delusional masking) of effects. And while some artists (quite rightly and smartly) choose to play into an effect to enhance the performance (and I admit to doing that, on a few cues in the tales), on the whole, I was focusing on the physical performance of my hands, saving digital effects for the mix to enhance the listener's experience.

A fuller context for this project's origin story is that we live in a digital age. It seems, with every passing week, there are dozens of tremendous guitarists who I've never heard of, showing up in my orbit. Never mind my own news feed — my wife's Spotify playlists also bring fresh stellar guitar playing into our lives. It's lovely — but like a lot of guitar players on this planet, the artistry of others becomes a bit mind-boggling, overwhelming, and deflating. Still — it also (eventually) fortifies my resolve to attempt to master my own domain, and not allow my admiration for others to damage my work ethic. (Eli silently reinforces the resolution.)

The tales shaped up more like song stories — miniatures — as opposed to vehicles for jazz chops I don't possess. Plus, those stereo chorus *Hejira* guitar sounds had influenced my early process. I wanted the guitar sound to start from simple and direct, then expand to get bigger — and wider. Pat Metheny, always one of my favourite guitar artists, had toured with Joni Mitchell in '79. Some speculate that Pat might have influenced Joni toward the idea of the Roland JC-120 stereo chorus amplifier (and the blonde George Benson archtop guitar she toured with.) Pat's own traditional rig spreads his guitar sound out across the stage. In my head, the compositions wouldn't balance out fully without some of the storytelling drama that special effects could provide. Bill Frisell was influential for some of that thinking, too.

To tell tales in my own way, I was going to need plug-ins — chorus, delays, reverbs, and the modulation of a few different phasers, flangers, and oscillators. I wasn't trying to disguise what was there musically, or compensate for things that were not. I applied production values to the audio in order to provide what the music was telling me would be complementary. Those who know their way around computer recording software might concur that this can present a series of Alice in Wonderland rabbit holes inside a Tardis. This veteran's solution: go with a gut-first instinct, or opt for simple, and move along.

In the ten tales, then, a listener encounters a layering of audio processing within a sound mix. (For more detailed notes see Blair Packham's descriptions in the addenda section at the end of the book.) Every song starts out with a clean guitar signal into a solid-state amp and a hint of the amp's digital plate reverb on the basic recording, which, I find, rounds out and warms up the bottom end of the guitar signal. At some point during mixing, in any given track, some subtle kind of chorusing might add some scope in stereo headphones. One of the plug-ins we used a lot was a Universal Audio Ocean Way simulator to ambient mic the original signal with virtual microphones placed at varying lengths down its cyber-room, to stereo it up. A second layer of reverb treatments might widen and space the atmosphere out even more. Phasing, flanging, rotary, or oscillating effects might give a "B" verse section or a chorus an auditory change of scenery. Echo or delay might enhance a bridge. As mentioned, Blair and I made these choices and decisions without too much time and energy spent on second-guessing. I wanted our mixing process to have something of a natural flow to it, not a laboured nitpicking. If it struck us with an appropriate delicious flavour, we went with it. Then Blair undertook a second wave of remixing to tweak details and clean up things that became evident after a mastering session. This necessitated a second mastering session done by Steve Skingley. In the end, I think the technology adds set design and drama to the simple storytelling of a solo electric fingerstyle guitar.

As always, beauty is in the eye of the beholder and the ear of the listener.

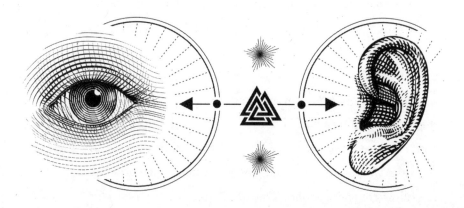

# 16

# WHY BOTHER?

———◆———

IN THE PREFACE TO HIS WONDERFUL BOOK, *WORLD WITHIN a Song*, Jeff Tweedy wrote:

> It'd be cool if we could see the worlds within the songs inside each other's heads. But I also love how impenetrable it all is. I love that what's mine can't be yours and we still get to call it ours. Songs are . . . the best way I know of to make peace with our lack of a shared consciousness.

At the end of the preface, he concludes:

> It's a joyous discovery to realize that something as ego-driven and interior as a book can return from its visit to all the people it managed to reach in the world with the hopeful and humbling message that you've been understood. You've given someone else the words to name their own experiences. Wonders never cease.

In my memoir, I went on (at length) about my reverence for music as a subjective experience while simultaneously being something that magically generates and enhances a sense of community. I agree with Mr. Tweedy — somehow, even after all is said and done, some of its mystery remains impenetrable. But I've written this book in the hope that it might make the music of these ten tales at least a bit more accessible.

Many times, I've written pieces of music with only an inarticulate instinct during creation, as facets of the piece remained abstruse, opaque — only to have the song reveal layers of itself over time.

Certainly, any songwriter will tell you that a song can take on more direction or meaning as an audience helps to breathe other unexpected layers of life into it.

Time is also a factor because music has the lovely ability to change and morph over the years so that it can embrace differences — maybe even more shades of meanings — than originally intended.

Maybe every creative act possesses this quality.

I've also quoted Mr. Tweedy because of the reference to his own book of prose, and the wonderful feedback he received from readers about what his organized words meant to them. In this, Tweedy's thoughts really resonated, bringing me back around to my own motives here. Throughout a lifetime of making recordings, I've sometimes had other folks engage in word-of-mouth about my work (when it was even noticed at all). Other times, I've had fans interpret the notes that flow through their heads, sparking imagination and generating dreams.

A quick 2024 Google search informs me that around 123,000 new songs are released each day. With all that music coming out through social media, news feeds, and the internet-driven culture we now have, snappy, insightful, provocative prose must show up as blurbs, tweets, teasers, revised biographies, and one-paragraph sell-sheet descriptions. Old-fashioned written words attempt to generate and capture public interest in the music, then fan it until videos go viral, converting the open-minded unaware through digital transmission. (*Telecasting!*)

In my typically 1436-Johannes-Gutenburg way of thinking, of course, I decided to write a book in some depth about the composing and recording process of an instrumental guitar record. (Makes complete modern sense to me.)

I couldn't imagine someone else bothering to do it. In any case, they could never have had the inside perspective that brought me to the table, to the laptop, to the *ego-driven* words *from the interior*, which you are now reading.

It led to a better understanding of my own motivations and process.

That made the exercise worthwhile.

# 17

## WHY TEN?

———◆———

W HY ARE THERE TEN TALES, NOT NINE OR ELEVEN? Was it purely for the alliteration of the title?

The answer is no. (Although I do like alliteration, as it contributes to catchy memorability. Which is why comic book writers like Jerry Siegel and Stan Lee created alliterative names for their principal characters.)

In my creative process, dozens of ideas fail to germinate. Of the ones that do, I still weed out things from the garden that might steal sunlight or choke out other plants that deserve the chance to grow and flower at a slower pace. In my sixth decade of making albums as a recording artist, I have a pretty strong instinct for the size and shape of a project and can begin to formulate a core at somewhere around five to seven pieces. Then I survey the crop, looking to complete the final harvest by supplementing and completing it with a satisfying range of feels, moods, keys, and tempos. I develop a sense of the overall shape of the project as it heads into its final creative phases (before actual pre-production rehearsing and demoing, and then the recording process itself).

"So Pushy" was the first piece that took on a life, which led me toward the idea of a whole album of fingerstyle electric guitar playing. The process of writing always goes by fits and starts, with some ideas dominating my attention for a period while others languish. Some arrive at a point where I have every confidence that I can bring 'em home with a few days of work, so then I usually shift my focus to others that need to be brought up to speed. Some iPhone voice memos never even qualify for secondary development. Some ideas die (as a few concepts for *The Barn Dance Suite* did) because, even after a fair amount of loving care and attention, they aren't differentiating themselves or demonstrating enough substance to earn more time.

On this project, that process got me to nine pieces. Then, from a few little chord progressions initially captured on my iPhone, I knew that (what has become) "Winter Nocturne" would be the appropriate closing track of the album. With it, I had ten musical stories to cover the territory I wanted to explore.

Still — why stop at ten? There's actually another solid, practical reason that serves as precedent.

When I was a young pup, signing my first recording deals and learning so many lessons the hard way, record companies had a standard clause in their contracts called the "controlled composition clause." If an artist recorded songs that they wrote themselves ("controlled" compositions), then the clause in the contract gave the record company the right to pay only a three-quarter mechanical royalty rate on those controlled compositions. In other words — you only got 75 percent of what they would pay out for songs written by outside writers. That clause went on to cap the number of payable compositions at ten. So, if you wrote and recorded eleven or twelve, well — great. But they were still only going to pay out on 75 percent of ten controlled compositions.

That became a standardized destination in my head. Ten original tracks satisfied the contractual obligation to the nasty, twisted, old music business. Force of habit — that's why I get to ten on the drawing board and my focus shifts from creative writing to pre-production.

# 18

# THE ABIDING GRACES

———◆———

ALL TEN INSTRUMENTAL GUITAR PIECES ARE CONSTRUCTED from the same dialect and vocabulary, yet differ in style. As their composer and performer, they all make very distinct and unique statements, to me. But after all's said and done, they're cumulative, ending up like an album of photographs from a journey, with a sum (hopefully) greater than its distinct, curated parts. My working theory is that the whole truth, and nothing but the truth, can generate meaningful benefits that spread out in different directions, creating their own reactions as the waves ripple out from the source.

> Love will not surrender to the pull of gravity
> Feeds the hunger of the tides that rise and fall
> Every ripple set in motion spreading into mystery
> Leaves me humble at the beauty of it all
> — RIK EMMETT, "THE LONGING," *The Spiral Notebook* ALBUM (1995)

In this lyric from way back, I was attempting to address and pack up a few things: human pursuits (songwriting and music making in particular), my own spirituality, and the love that feeds creativity. Twenty-nine years have passed since I wrote those words. During the rising and falling of the tides in late 2023, I was attempting to tell ten tales via solo electric guitar. But my sense of longing had not changed. Neither had my humility in the face of love, except perhaps that it has grown deeper, larger. I hope and trust that the gift of life and the blessing of love is ever-present in the music I keep trying to offer.

———•———

This brings me around to a promise made back in the "Layers" chapter — a discussion about emotion.

———•———

We're also going to graduate from the very human, primal, fundamental "duality" I'd mentioned earlier (and summoned Leonard Bernstein to articulate and endorse), up to the triangulations that Mr. Bernstein ascribed to the mysticism of the Holy Trinity.

Love is the foundation of emotion, which is the third element in the musician's eternal triangle of intellectual, physical, and emotional. One good triangle deserves another — and if these three elements are working well together, they generate a fourth component — the *spiritual*. The foundation of almost everything I've ever done as an artist is based on faith, hope, and love — the abiding graces. (As I see it, even my anger arises out of frustrated love.)

As any writer can tell you, eternal triangulations generate plenty of potential for tension. It can get messy. The spiritual can lead into supernatural territory. Later on, in relation to my reggae tune "Burlytown," I'll reference Stephen Marley's take on integrity. An ethical, humanist side to spirituality has always worked for me as both rocket fuel and lubricant in the creative process. For the sake of simplicity here, I'd prefer to categorize all things that arise from human imagination as intellectual, to try and keep a lid on the Pandora's Box of the "supernatural." There's no denying the messy chaos of human curiosity, ingenuity, and emotion. There's no containing it, either.

On the surface, a collection of instrumental guitar pieces may not seem to carry a lot of weighted depth. For some, all this talk about spirit, intellect, and emotion probably doesn't jibe. Nevertheless, I felt inclined to unpack my ten tales to see if readers might agree with the poetic faith and secondary belief that I imagined was instilled in them.

Consider these ten pieces as avatars seeking a vibe — music, ringing out, hoping for listeners who might find their imaginations captured. Given how the dynamics of spirituality work for us human beings, with our works of art representational and metaphorical in nature, "virtual" realities are created to try and make sense of our nature in this universe. Sometimes our vision becomes *telescopic* and wide-ranging. In the case of these instrumental pieces, they began with a fair bit of *microscopic* researching, mostly because there's only one track of guitar playing as content — but also, as I worked up the music (and because I'd been writing books of poetry, and a memoir), I began seriously entertaining the notion of writing this companion book. I just kept adjusting the focus on the electron microscope, as the annoying little kid inside me kept asking,

"Why? But . . . *why?*"

(The end product itself actually goes to motive, your honour.)

———•———

I once wrote a lyric in the song "Ask," on an album entitled *Good Faith*:

> *It's a question of want — It's a question of need*
> *It's the way we figure out the things we choose to believe*
> *and it's a measure of faith and it's a question of trust*
> *and there's an answer for you and me — and the answer is us.*

All of our questions about want and need eventually lead to choices we make, based on our intellectual and emotional inner explorations. Often, in the end, we say that we eventually rely on our "gut instincts" — what feels right for us. Artists use their human imagination to explore, trying to "capture" the imaginations of others.

Centuries ago, the live performances of troubadours and court musicians tried to conjure that vibe. Now, in our digital universe, boundaries have long been breached so that virtual experiences can lead us to make gut-instinct choices about the life within and without, inside us, and surrounding us.

Vibe equals gut instinct: reactions based on emotional kinds of responses.

I'm still trying to wrap my head around the vast implications, consequences, and potential of virtual digital experiences and artificial intelligence. Meanwhile, I found myself creating ten pieces, recording them digitally, disseminating them in a universe of ones and zeroes, then sitting in front of my laptop and typing words into a software program so that I might enhance the digital experience — bring added value to supplement it, enlighten, expand, enhance, and *illuminate*. (My tangential mind just conjured a row of twelfth-century monks seated at the cold windows in the "cells" of a scriptorium, working on illuminated texts of Biblical content. At least I have the creature comforts of Eli's Loft.)

When I write and record an album of music, I have to confront my own hypocrisy, sense of morality, and humanity — my take on good and bad faith. All these matter to me, far beyond any standard commercial transaction of generating a product for the marketplace. Whatever else it might represent, *Ten Telecaster Tales* stands as a portrait of Rik Emmett, from 2021 to 2024. And just who is that old guy becoming now, anyway?

Ah — progress or regress? Evolution or devolution? (Joni Mitchell's "Both Sides Now": *"Something's lost, and something's gained, in living every day."*) There's a bit of a paradox in the matrix of this. I mean — I'm inside the work, and as much as I'd love to be able to get outside it and walk around it and give it the 360, there's always some of me still inside it, which I can't deny.

I once drew a cartoon for *Hit Parader* magazine showing a giant, larger-than-life Gene Simmons of Kiss performing; then in a subsequent panel, a little hatch door has swung open on the back, and a little man in his underwear is popping out.

That "Wizard of Oz" dynamic is present in the inceptions of creativity. I write and record music so that I can put some of myself into something larger than my life, live through something beyond me, and — hopefully — so that folks can find parts of things that capture their imagination. There's a lot of hope in what I offer up; there's a ton of good faith, and it's a labour of love, I assure you. That's on the artsy, "dreaming big dreams" side of the equation.

On the nuts-and-bolts side of the crafting, I can report that when I make a recording and struggle to generate the best take I can muster, I'm happy to apply any new tools at my disposal for the capturing of imagination. Why wouldn't I exercise every resource in hopes of capturing the imaginations of others?

This capacity for toolmaking might have arisen in the evolving minds of *homo habilis*, becoming a watershed development toward what makes us human. (Cue Stanley Kubrick's iconic *2001: A Space Odyssey* bone-discovered-to-be-a-useful-weapon / tool, tossed and floating skyward in slow motion, abruptly hard-edited into a floating spaceship.)

Consequently, full disclosure: yes, on *Ten Telecaster Tales*, we used digital editing to solve some of my personal problems in the capturing of the content.

Generously, that might suggest an older artist's "Glenn Gould" tendencies to *perfect* the recording. However, when feeling less highfalutin and a mite pricklier, I'd grumble that it was necessary simply to make the content *palatable*. It became apparent that my romantic notions going in, of capturing the pieces "live off the floor" in complete takes, would have to acquiesce to the wonders of Digital Performer editing software (with Universal Audio hardware/plug-ins) as essential and integral to the process.

—— • ▸ ——

A lifelong habit and comforting ritual cycle of creativity drove my desire to write. After that — why choose to learn, record, and share this particular collection of guitar pieces? In a narrow sense, I wanted to express something about a certain kind of guitar, within my certain style of guitar playing. My guts convinced me that this deep-dive exercise in self-indulgence amounted to more than just another vanity project.

As I age, of course, my guts aren't all that reliable. I harbour no illusions about the fact that it is, obviously, naturally, and unmistakably, a very self-indulgent autobiographical vanity project. Still, way down deep from the bottom of my heart, a tiny candle somehow manages to keep sending out its rays of hope — its vibe. In a much wider sense, I hope that the music will matter to other folks. That feeling of hope is tied to the authenticity and integrity that I try to write into the tunes, and then develop through the expression of my performance technique.

*Vibe.*

Almost always, I've wanted my musical creations to be *about* something — not just celebrating the simplicity of the music, in the moment, but representative of other layers. That wider, deeper something is the eternal search for the ring of truth — that resonance in our gut instincts, in our lizard brains, the brain stem, cerebellum, and basal ganglia.

Art is life, reflecting it like a mirror — capturing it. It makes observations about life and, in so doing, takes on a kind of life of its own.

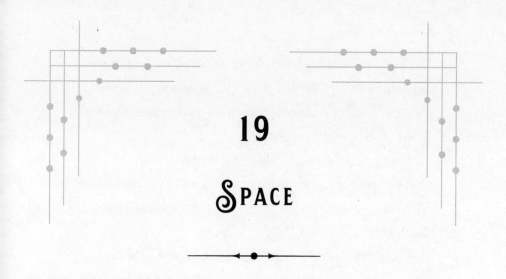

# 19

# §PACE

*We're all just strangers here . . .*
*Groping in the darkness*
*searching for a way*
*To fill the empty space inside*
*And between us all.*

— TRIUMPH, "STRANGER IN A STRANGE LAND," *Thunder Seven* ALBUM (1984)

THIS IS WHAT MUSIC DOES: IF WE LET IT, IT FILLS THE AIR. It can bridge the space between us and inside us — help us to connect to others and our own emotions. It can set the mood, aiding and abetting communion, which is why it's such a valuable component of religious and political services, football stadium events, and mall shopping.

In my life, I've managed to make music of many styles and kinds. Some of it has done those things mentioned above.

But here I have decided to make an album of *solo instrumental fingerstyle electric* guitar. Via those four modifying adjectives, I willingly sliced my demographic audience down into microscopic slivers of the general population.

Can't help it. The music made me do it.

This topic of *space* will arise again later, in the tale of the "Allemande." But I want to examine the subject in some depth here.

The catalogue of music that I'd already made in my life imposed upon the tales' agenda. That force works in many mysterious ways. It generates a "been there, done that" factor (a thing to avoid) but also provides a comfort factor, which invites evolution or creative variations on a theme. The dynamic of familiarity can give the revisions of history an attractive appeal. I didn't fight it. I embraced the past, welcoming it and working with it in the my present space.

At the age of seventy, the space inside my head hisses and whistles with tinnitus. My immediate surrounding space generates less inclination to have other musicians add their decibels to the mix. Drawn toward quiet elbow room, a solo record of instrumentals felt entirely logical and natural.

But — as a guy accustomed to vocals, band tracks, and the dynamics of ensemble work — the question then became, how is one lonely guitar going to provide enough drama? The answer to that is also — *space*. The stereo spectrum provides *width*; reverb, echo, and effects generate *depth*.

Colour. *Energy.* **Size.** $D_i{}^m{}_n sio^n$.

The making of music inherently challenges the balancing of macro and micro within the *space* of the work. The composition of that work rests on thousands of arbitrary choices and decisions. (Neil Peart coined it so well: "If you choose not to decide, you still have made a choice.") The space that gets defined by those choices seeks to deliver the perfect balance between whatever is in motion, moving outside in and inside out.

Just as the judicious application of effects raises multiple dimensions of space within the limited confines and context of a Telecaster guitar album, other aspects of generating space in a song can come from the composition itself. Developing a song's form, I often employ "B" verses (or pre-choruses) and bridges — sections of songs that open them up and grow them, providing fresh vitality to the proceedings. And just as the space of a song can expand, it can shrink. A re-intro resets the space and brings it back closer to its baseline. Additionally, a coda that gives off every impression of bringing things to a close prepares the listener for the approaching limits of the space.

A tempo might remain metronomically steady in composition (even quantized). Yet events can occur musically within the structures to accelerate or decelerate the proceedings. Moments where the forward motion slows into a *rubato* feel, or the music hits a *fermata* point. Chord changes can start happening faster and more often, adding energy; or they can stretch out and make the material feel more ponderous and relaxed. Melodies can start taking on more notes, getting shorter and more emphatic, or could even disappear for periods, generating a sense of resting, breathing,

*ssssssssslllllllooowwwwwwwinnggggg dowwwwwwwwwnnnnn.*
The accordioning of content generates its own sense of space.

———————•—•———————

Songwriter Neil Finn of Crowded House offered one brilliant definition of space in the opening two lyric lines of "Don't Dream It's Over":

> *There is freedom within*
> *There is freedom without*

It's been said that space is the "final frontier." Not to quibble with *Star Trek* writer Samuel Peeples (whose opening monologue subsequently passed through a steering committee of series creator Gene Roddenberry and producers John D.F. Black and Bob Justman), but I'm tempted to argue that a bold adventure happens every time the music originating from the infinities inside *my* imagination gets into the cochlea of someone else, heading up their auditory nerve toward the infinities of *their* imagination.

Submitted, for your consideration: the potential variations of our inner explorations are as infinite as the vast expanses of the heavenly galaxies.

———•◦•———

There are frontiers in every open mind.

———•◦•———

What I currently find particularly compelling about *space* is that my *time* to generate creative bold adventures is finite, and the end of my own *space in time* has been inexorably drawing itself into consideration. And while *Ten Telecaster Tales*, in and of itself, may seem a humble enough undertaking and public offering, it felt like it was the right thing at the right time in the right place.

My optimism would have led me to believe that, going into almost all of the creative projects in my lifetime. But it's not necessarily how I might describe what they look like in a rearview mirror.

There's a whole space-time continuum thing, and with this project, I was really feeling it.

After completing the mix/mastering of the tales, there's yet another perspective of time that presented itself. Way back when I started writing the pieces, I had vague notions of what I hoped to achieve and began to seek hints from within the ideas that were on the table. Imagine a sculptor, walking 360 degrees around the stone, waiting for it to suggest *what needs to be taken away* in order to let the art within the rock emerge. It takes time to explore space, and those considerations give you a sense of whether or not the shape of your ideas works appropriately. After giving it some space and time, the tales felt complete enough that I could move on.

In the final stages of redecorating our renovated home, my wife Jeannette and I commissioned the wonderful artist Floyd Elzinga to create a triptych surrounding the mantel and fireplace on the east wall of our dining room. We had familiarized ourselves with his body of work as a metal sculptor, his wall art rendered in wonderful 3D layers of treated metals. I did up some sketches, and we took some photos of the space, to give him a sense of what we envisioned. He remarked (as polite conversation) that we'd already done a lot of the work. I replied, "As an artist myself, I know full well that your process relies on what the metal says to you as you work the pieces up. What we've done is just preliminary prep. We're commissioning you for your interpretation of what the metal is suggesting and offering to you, in your process."

And we're delighted afresh every day with what he delivered.

Time gives distance. Space allows for a calm consideration of *feel*. That's artistic process.

The music of the tales developed, giving me clues to what it could become. Gradually, I fashioned the pieces into forms that I began to get to know and rehearse, realizing that one of the strongest sub-themes of the tales is that these stories owed so much to other narratives from my past, offering fresh perspectives on territory staked out long ago.

> *And all the lines being drawn*
> *Become a question of degrees*
>
> — RIK EMMETT, "THOSE SHOES," *Live at Berklee* ALBUM (2000)

Stories shift by questions of degrees because the world has altered. The listener has changed; the storyteller has aged. This artist has absorbed a lot more experience, sporting his scars and bruises from the school of hard knocks. Maybe there's some wisdom gained. Maybe it's just that senses have dulled, ambition has mellowed, and agendas have shifted. But the drawing of solid lines isn't as boldly and hastily executed. The lines can be vague, shifting on the blowing sand; they're hardly ever straight. (Unless the gut insists that they absolutely *must* be.)

I'd like to believe that, if we possess enough common sense, the Golden Rule eventually teaches us to cut other folks plenty of slack because we require it for ourselves. Conversely, my common sense has taught me to give a wide berth to folks lacking in understanding, equanimity, compassion, and empathy. My stories seek those who take a generosity of spirit into account.

I compose music because it's a delivery platform for emotion and thought provocation. But the songs become living, breathing things of their own, redrawing creative and philosophical lines.

In his memoir, *Making It So*, the acclaimed actor Patrick Stewart reveals that his education at the Bristol Old Vic Theatre School, followed by his time in the Royal Shakespeare Company in the '60s, locked him into a mistaken mindset, that there was only one "right" way to perform a role.

"I thought it was my duty to deliver the exact same performance, show after show."

Why was that attitude and belief wrong-headed?

"I was denying the audience a unique experience . . ."

As the composer, then performer of the Ten Telecaster Tales, I was walking a line suspended between two points. At one end, the written work was a script that needed to be solid enough to establish the delivery platform, providing the performer with the necessary support and tools to do the job. There's no question in my mind that the writer's script needs to be respected. But at the other end — every performance has the potential to be unique. What's in the air? Who's listening? What day of the week is it? What kinds of emotions are percolating in me right now? (What did I have for lunch?) This is very much about finding what's right for the space, on the time continuum.

My experience, as both a composer and performer, had led me to this — these moments in time — the creation and execution of the tales. I wanted them to possess the mature wisdom and understanding of the suspended tightrope between disciplines.

This is something I'd sussed intuitively as a teenager when I wrote a poem in high school:

> *Music holds the secret*
> *To know it can make you whole*
> *It's not just a game of notes*
> *It's the sounds inside your soul.*

That poem found new life in the song "Hold On," which appeared on Triumph's *Just a Game* album in 1979. Once again, in December 2023, I found myself trying to work out music's secrets, playing the game of notes I held in my hands, employing my head and heart while attempting to capture the sounds inside my seventy-year-old soul.

Just like Patrick Stewart, I had to relearn the lesson that it's supposed to be about "play." The "game" element lives in the moment. I literally get to hold the moment in my hands.

Time — and *space*.

*Time in space — space in time.*

What am I to do about that?

———— ◆ ▸ ————

Months of pre-production — writing and rehearsing — led to a point where I felt enough confidence to begin recording. I'd love to say that I had the pieces perfectly memorized by that point, but that's not the way repertoire lives in my head anymore. My memory is not as reliable and resilient as it used to be. Every time I play new songs, parts of them remain alive and elusive, and any part of them might suggest something different, something new. Something might confound me afresh or escape my mental command or physical control, and I'll have to readdress the music and rework it.

So that stage of the process took its own sweet time. Eventually, I started to move past the organization of notes and phrases and think in detail about how the music *should* sound. And that revealed even more depth as I tried to understand how we should produce the actual recorded sound of it and the texture of the audio space that it would inhabit.

After that, we finally started mastering the mixed recordings we had made, and the music still had things it could and did reveal. All of the time these stages of development took reminds me of a lesson relearned with every recording project I undertake: time is fluid. It will *always* keep running, and the music will keep offering me insights about what it was, what it is, and what it can be.

Time will continue to pass. I will change. Life will vary. The air that carries the music will transform. And the music will shift, too. The Telecaster Tales will continue to teach me about myself and my guitar playing, about my music and my life.

That's just another story, inside the stories, inside this book about the music of *Ten Telecaster Tales*.

———•——

Alright — enough with the preamble. Let's shift our focus in Part Two to an investigation of the tales, one by one.

# Part Two

---◆---

# Ten Telecaster Tales

THE TEN TELECASTER TALES ARE


1. SO PUSHY

2. FUNKY SCRATCHIN'


*THE BARN DANCE SUITE*

3. SWIRLING

(COURANTE)

4. ALLEMANDE

5. COWBOY AND GAUCHO WALTZ

(VALSE A RASGUEADO)


6. SLINKY

7. BURLYTOWN

8. THE RIO GLIDE

9. GEE WHIZ

10. WINTER NOCTURNE


*"THIS KIND"*

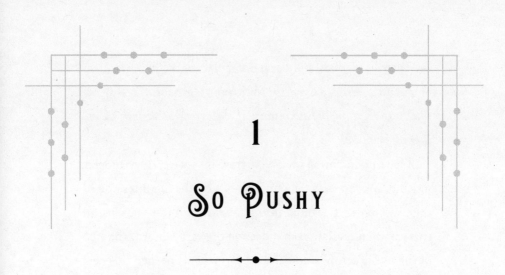

# 1

# So Pushy

*Wait — did you hear that?*
*Oh, this is sure stirring up some ghosts for me.*
— ROBBIE ROBERTSON, "SOMEWHERE DOWN THE CRAZY RIVER" (1987)

"SO PUSHY" WAS A POINT OF ORIGIN, WHERE THIS WHOLE package of musical storytelling began. I did a work-up of a short sketch that had previously been a solitary twelve-bar jazz-blues segue piece in the audiobook for my poetry collection, *Reinvention*, turning it into a full tune.

This first story introduces the main characters, sets the time and place, and, hopefully, provokes questions that raise interest in some archaeology, digging down deep to find some answers. Two of those main characters are Richard Gordon Emmett and his Telecaster guitar, Babs.

The time is 2022 and 2023, but as James Baldwin put it so eloquently, *"History is not the past. It is the present. We carry our history with us. We are our history. If we pretend otherwise, we are literally criminals."*

I have no intention of *stealing* from my own history. Indeed, much of the ten tales' content comes with the full intention of acknowledging it, leaning into it, *counting* on it — not just in these written revelations but deep in the very fabric of the vibe of the music composition and performance. I needed this new music to speak in the language of my roots — the stuff I was learning back in 1968 through 1973. Especially in this piece, "So Pushy," I went looking for updates on the licks and phrasing that I was discovering as a teenager.

The baggage of my career lives in my present work — monogrammed luggage, all custom-built. My way of handling identity is not to deny it but own it — take advantage of it. Get up on those suitcases. Use 'em as soapboxes. Raise up new music so the tunes can carry, straight at whoever's listening.

Let my baggage inform the present: morph it, evolve it, shape-shift it. It's only one of the infinitely beautiful, manifold things that music can do.

Pushy? I'm pushing the envelope in a lot of directions. One of those directions tries to turn back the clock. Yet in the next few bars, I'm right back in the present, trying to push across a bar line. (The old guy's still in *such a hurry* to get to the future.)

As for setting the place, an obvious answer is Eli's Loft, my home studio, with a Shure 57 microphone slightly off-axis on the speaker of the amp.

It's also set in the burly town of Burlington, Ontario, Canada. This is where I live, and I hope that listeners can hear the accent of this location in the music that I make.

But in more esoteric ways, "place" is also very much the narrowing world of an old rock star learning how to manage the third act of his life. He's getting to feel like he knows his place. He can hear it in the air of comfortable humility, moderate expectations, and the acceptance of diminished returns. It's a place where he doesn't want to rest too long or too easily on laurels and doesn't want to appear to be (with double apologies to Paul Simon) an old pony turning the same old singular trick, like *a cartoon in a cartoon graveyard*.

The place of this particular "So Pushy" track — of this whole album — is actually a *bunch* of locations. It's the bedroom of 94 Abbott Avenue in West Toronto, where I learned and practised guitar as a kid in the late '60s and early '70s. It's the "man-cave" of Rik Weiditch's house on Indian Road, where my teenage head and heart were introduced to the roots of great guitar playing. It's the basements of houses and churches and the High Park YMCA of Toronto, where I practised and rehearsed with baby bands.

I was never a teenager who felt like there was nothing to do or no particular place to go. I could always pick up a guitar or try to get together with someone and make some music.

Another one of the places of any recording is inside the artist's head.

From its humble origin, I knew this single twelve-bar verse of jazzy blues would require variations on the theme from verse to verse. It also took on a Lenny Breau lick (that I learned from Alf Cormier in a portable at Parkdale Collegiate while gainfully employed in the summer of '71 at an Opportunities for Youth music workshop), which I've used numerous times in compositions.

The shades of blue in the territory between the fourth and fifth notes of a scale have never lost their appeal to me. Another fairly standard compositional device shows up in this piece (as it does in many of these tales) — a chordal tritone substitution, as the dominant V7 (an altered E7) shifts to a Bb7b5 chord. The indigo grease of this turn reoccurs in other tales — in "Funky Scratchin'"; a great deal in "Slinky"; and even in "The Rio Glide" — staking out an Emmett-ism that can be traced back to other guitar work in my past ("Knuckleball Sandwich," "Taste of Steel," "Woke Up This Morning," et cetera).

Once the chromaticism of a walking-bass line makes voice-leading suggestions, they're hard to overlook.

The eight-bar "B" section of "So Pushy" grew out of an urge to work a contrasting section off of the IV chord, Dm. That eight-bar "B" happens twice, with the second variation leading me up the neck and into yet another variation of the turnaround.

———•———

Here's a tangent about *urges*. I can't articulate where they come from. Creative urges are a part of my nature, and when things are going well, there seems an inexhaustible supply, with a fair number of the urges proving useful. Some folks might attribute creative urges to supernatural, mystical powers, but I tend to think it's just human trial and error.

Consider: .303 is the median batting average of major league players who make it to the Baseball Hall of Fame. The average everyday major leaguer hits around .250. Now — you might still hold on to your MLB contract if your batting average drops to .200, but after a while — *probably not*.

To me, that range defines the creative ballpark (so to speak) of urges. Creative urges don't pan out *somewhere between* seven and eight times out of ten.

Not to worry. I once hosted a college seminar where I interviewed the famous Canadian record producer Bob Ezrin. I asked about songwriter credits and the sometimes-awkward negotiation of royalty shares — carving Solomon's baby up over original song ideas and contributions. Ezrin shared his father's wise counsel on generosity (a variation of Richard Branson's famous quote about business opportunities). Ezrin's dad told him: be generous with good ideas, because they're like subway trains. If you miss one, don't worry. Another one will be coming along shortly.

*All in good time.*

I try to remember this advice when things aren't going well, and my creative urges don't seem very creative. *Or urgent.* Don't worry — just keep goin' up to the plate and takin' your hacks. Eventually, some will start falling in for you.

In the baseball movie *Bull Durham*, scripted by Ron Shelton, the veteran minor-league catcher Crash Davis (after a few beers) is explaining to rookie phenom Nuke LaLoosh the difference between success and failure:

*You know what the difference between hitting .250 and .300 is? It's 25 hits. Twenty-five hits in 500 at-bats is 50 points, OK? There's six months in a season. That's about 25 weeks. That means if you get just one extra flare a week, just one, a gork, a ground ball — a ground ball with eyes! — you get a dying quail, just one more dying quail a week, and you're in Yankee Stadium. You still don't know what I'm talking about, do you?*

I know exactly what Crash was talking about, because I've been a creative artist all my life. Sometimes an urge leads to a dying quail, and *whaddayaknow?* — you're off to the races.

———— • ————

Thanks for indulging the tangent: back to the structure of "So Pushy." Despite the developments of variations in the verse and "B" sections, I felt there was still something missing in the piece's entirety. I kept thinking: *This thing still needs more attitude, like the kinda riff Billy Gibbons or Jimmy Page would add.* That last urgent piece (which completed the puzzle I was constructing in my head) dropped into place when this ditty acquired its rock/blues head riff. Once I had the three successive slight variations of the riff worked out, it took on a fancy-pants, Chuck-Berry-ish lick, to cap off the eight-bar section. This could then recur in the arrangement to reset the proceedings and ground its jazzy flights of harmonic fancy.

———— • ————

Okay, but beyond these insights into the invention of the architecture — what's really going on here, personally?

The music is about a restless urge to push across bar lines and anticipate downbeats. The artist is the protagonist in this story. I can't help myself, getting out ahead of the way things are running in real time, so full of eager ambition and the prime directive of my DNA to compete, procreate, evolve, and mutate, as the juice of my consciousness and the rocket fuel of ego combine to drive the firetruck (and occasionally cheat a rolling stop at the four-way signs).

A gift like that can be a blessing when it bestows a competitive edge. But it's also a curse that places an Achilles-heel target directly in my blind spot. The older I get, the more I feel I have to keep that target moving. But now I lack both the quickness of speedy reflexes and my confidence in them. So that's partly what this rhythm and blues is — the soundtrack of a moving target, coming to terms.

A man of many contradictions attempts to sit in the pocket of his Telecaster, yet enjoys pushing across bar lines. Consequently, he also has to constantly remind himself not to rush; just sit back and let the tempo pull him along. That persistent insistence is always a part of his overall story — a motivation for propulsion, for *emotion in motion under locomotion*. That tendency, even at a metronomic, quantized tempo — that threat of acceleration, that *pushiness* — sometimes makes him start cutting checks he won't be able to cash. (By the way — amongst musicians, this is widely perceived as one of the common traits of guitarists in general.)

But can't that also be a good thing? Restlessness can also be salvation because it's also motivation to walk away from games at unwinnable tables. Sometimes, it keeps me from drowning — like a shark that must keep moving, forcing the oxygen in the water through my gills. Aggression and ambition got me noticed, edging on out ahead of the pack.

The thing about tendencies: it's good to be self-aware, and work with whatever comes naturally, trying to harness the value, and downplay the liability.

This particular piece of music has a lot of two-fret slides written into it. In terms of gross motor control, my left-handedness on the fretboard dominates. That power lets me get *greasy* (at least, that's how it sounds and feels to me). Meanwhile, adding a lot of *spank* and *snap* into the right-hand picking balances out the playing field and plays right into the character of a Telecaster.

On playback, that's the kind of stuff I hear. There's just enough ambience added to the mix that a short glissando on the low string of the guitar sounds a bit like a growl, which I find satisfying. It's in keeping with the rest of that Telly attitude.

I'll venture that good rocking should always have some swing in it — informing it — the energy threatening to skip up into triplets or sextuplets at the slightest provocation. It makes the music compelling, even a bit dangerous, like an accident about to happen any second. It might come off the rails, like a horrifying train wreck. (Can you avert your gaze? Turn your head away?)

Even when the game plan is to stick to a twelve-bar of jazzy R&B, the rocker in me can't help himself. Other parts start popping out of the form — the train's momentum squeals against the track — raising the ante, and the proceedings go up the neck another octave.

What am I trying to prove by pushing this agenda?

Well — my chi, the energy within me, pursues the chi that lives in the guitar. I keep imagining a sweet spot where the two chis integrate. *It's just out ahead of me. Keep pushing.*

Another part of me has decided to try and prove that the best way forward is to own my urges — incorporate 'em, take advantage of 'em, harness 'em, follow 'em on down the tried and true-blue pathways of pentatonic shapes and patterns, establishing a solid little foundational creation myth with its own dynamics, in its own time and place.

Maybe the thin line of the present is like a tightrope, stretched between what threatens to be cliché from the past, across to a future where people will eventually hear these original compositions, captured as recordings, representing a seventy-year-old guitarist at a balanced point along his own timeline.

(And dig it.)

Ahh — maybe I'm pushy, but there's that carrot out there pulling me: the acceptance of *strangers.* Ambition — *pride* — you devilish thing.

Some might wonder (just like yours truly) why there has always been this need to be so *pushy.*

I'm answering that now with a bit of a shrug, and an admission that I'm always trying to settle down these natural impulses. I made the Telecaster Tales to see if I could put some old ghosts to rest.

That's the subtext of this allegorical yarn. Knit one, purl ten.

———◄•►———

AND SO, THE TALES HAVE BEGUN.

# SO PUSHY
## 8 BARS.

INTRO
E G A

12 BARS

V1     variation — slide at $F\triangle^7$ VIII → X → VIII

V2   12 BARS    variation → $F\triangle^7$ — Dials down from V

2 STRING TURNY LICK <sup>LOW</sup> <sub>DOWN</sub> INTO $Dm^7$ [DOWN] → variation $F\triangle^7$ →
V3                                       SOFT harmony TURN
                                        OPEN STRINGS

2 STRING TURNY LICK <sup>HIGH</sup> <sub>up</sub> INTO $Dm^7$ [up]
V4            Build into ENERGY STRUMS

REINTRO 8 BARS

DYNAMICS DOWN
V5 (SOFT START)   same as first → $F\triangle^7$ slide VIII X VIII

— 2 STRING TURNY LICKS — LOW — HIGH

ENDING — Muted RUN up to TURNY LICK at XVII

CHUCK BERRY LICK at XX

$Am^9$ open B

FAN

NOTES
— 4 $F\triangle^7$ turns → — Hi Slide → V dials down
→ I soft turn
— Hi Slide again

— emphasize dynamics

# 2

# FUNKY SCRATCHIN'

———— •‣• ————

*For many of us just starting to play during [the '60s and '70s], Domenic [Troiano] and his customized Telecaster were highly influential and literally held in awe! Donnie played with an intensity and emotion that set him apart from an entire generation of guitarists . . . immersed in the city's burgeoning rock and R&B music culture, along with other budding guitar slingers, [he] used to study The Hawks' Robbie Robertson at The Concord Tavern Saturday matinees. . . . He defined what contemporaries call "The Toronto Sound" during stints with Robbie Lane and The Disciples . . . and by replacing Robbie Robertson in the lead guitar role with Ronnie Hawkins.*

— 12FRET.COM

IN 1960S TORONTO, THERE WERE AS MANY FUNKY R&B bands as there were rock groups — maybe more. Certainly, the primo hotshot Telly guitarist was Robbie Robertson. Then Domenic Troiano followed, who became legendary for the rootsy R&B feel that animated and informed his stylings of rock 'n' roll. Robertson was a bit before my time (although I heard some stories), but Troiano's reputation enjoyed hot currency.

In those days, an up-and-coming multi-threat guitarist needed to capture the vibes of Motown's Joe Messina, Robert White, Eddie Willis, and Dennis Coffey; the Stax/Volt presence of Steve Cropper; the country of James Burton; and the funk of Jimmy Nolen (from James Brown's band). Jimi Hendrix evolved the influence of Curtis Mayfield, and while psychedelic virtuosity gained Jimi massive, iconic popularity, it was his rhythmic musicality that helped to define his style.

— • —

Rhythm — it's the key. *Rhythm rules as king.*

— • —

On the Telecaster named Babs (which sports the string plane, scale length, and dual humbucker pickups of a Les Paul), I just slip the selector switch into its middle position and modify my self-taught rasgueado technique to get into funky scratchin' mode. It gives off a *liquid* sound. The bookend opening and closing licks are in the style of country pickers like Albert Lee and Jerry Reed. Right off the bat, it establishes an aggressive in-yer-face presence.

In particular, Reed's influential piece "The Claw" first came to me from a recording of Lenny Breau's, but I favoured Chet

Atkins's version. (I don't think it's possible to make a modern fingerstyle guitar record that won't have Atkins's fingerprints and DNA all over it.) In a way, I think ambitious guitarists of my era viewed "The Claw" as something of an entrance exam. If you couldn't cut a version of it, you could never get past the front gates of the Guitar Club.

Once the verses kick in, I'm sliding ninth chords around, and hammering on thirds and sixth chords, just like all those dudes I name-dropped a few paragraphs ago. This tune lives in the land of country major pentatonic. The challenge remains: can you find something original to say, speaking a language that has already been so eloquently and totally covered?

A couple of thoughts immediately bounce back at me.

1. Shakespeare was a pretty good playwright. Didn't stop folks from trying their hand at writing amazing plays. (Novels. Poems. Screenplays. Blogs. *TikTok slogans.*)
2. What was it that C.S. Lewis wrote?

    *Even in literature and art, no man who bothers about originality will ever be original: whereas if you simply try to tell the truth (without caring two pence how often it has been told before) you will, nine times out of ten, become original without ever having noticed it.*

———•——

Awright, Clive Staples.

———•——

Your mission, Richard Gordon, should you choose to accept it: put your own heart and soul and hands and head into the work, and then just let it speak for itself. (Plus — write an accompanying book sharing your roots and the torturous rationalizing you put yourself through, and type out every single goddamn crazy tangential angle on the material that seems even remotely plausible.)

The goal of "Funky Scratchin'" was to pick up a torch that Robertson and Troiano brandished in the Toronto scene, six decades ago, and carry on that flame. This philosophical approach to my guitar playing — picking up on traditional bloodlines and trying to contribute to their evolution — is not new to me, either. I made an album in 1993 called *Ipso Facto* (which subsequently suffered a mostly unheralded death), featuring a lot of eclectic songs about guitar playing — shredding hard rock, blues, folk, and jazz. A psychedelic rock song on there called "Rainbow Man" described guitar heroism via the electric church of a Jimi Hendrix character, which contained this spoken word poem:

> *Targets moving in the magnetic pull of truth*
> *Forever restless to regain love's living proof*
> *Brokering emotions as only dreamers can*
> *Measuring the universe in terms they understand*
> *When the colour gun fires in the hands of a rainbow man*

To this Toronto kid, in the '6os, the first and most accessible Rainbow Men were two guitar hotshots from Rompin' Ronnie Hawkins' band — Robbie and Donnie. And here Rikky is, five decades later, still restless, still brokering and measuring, 2023-style.

But instead of firin' off a colour gun, this time around it's funky, and I'm *scratchin'* it.

SCRATCHIN'

# THE BARN DANCE SUITE

## 3

## SWIRLING

### (COURANTE)

———◆→———

*Life in us is like the water in a river.*

— HENRY DAVID THOREAU

THE BARN DANCE SUITE WAS NOT A CHUNK OF WRITING that came along sequentially. Actually, once the Telecaster Tales began (many of them on a Godin Supreme, actually, as your storyteller waited on delivery of the new swamp ash and maple "telecasting" device), a scattered grouping of riffs and ideas were transcribed from iPhone voice memos and scribbled into a spiral notebook: specifically, the beginnings of "Slinky," "Burlytown," and "Gee Whiz." But then, along came a commission to create an original bourrée for a documentary film. That ensemble recording, with drums, bass, and overdubs, didn't suit my projected vision for The Tales, of purely solo pieces. But then one thing kept leading to another, and the germs of a make-believe suite started showing up.

Later in the process, trying to make a logical sense of the sequence of the ten tales, the *courante* was placed ahead of the *allemande*, which preceded the *valse*.

There's a solid historical origin story for imagining a dance suite. At Christmas in 1968, my brother Rob gave me a magical and influential copy of Julian Bream playing Bach's Lute Suites 1 and 2 — so I know it's cheeky to call what I've done a "suite." It gives it a frame of window-dressing, but form-wise, that's just a figment of my own associative thinking — or perhaps apophenia.

Upon reflection, I can only suggest that (a) the energy of the three pieces felt logical in this order, and (b) they all have eighteenth-century dance grooves. It also might bear mentioning that along the way, a fourth dance suite piece bit the dust, proving to be a rabbit hole too deep. (*For now.*) So as suites go, yes — my little barn dance one is a mite thin. But these three ideas were, simply, the ones that survived the creative process. (As a senior citizen, I remain keen on survival as a modest victory in itself.)

———•—————

One more chunk of insight: earlier on, I referenced Leonard Bernstein's take on "duality" evolving into the "mysticism" of music based on things happening in the Holy Trinity of triple meter. In the Barn Dance Suite of my Tales, the *courante* flows in a six-eight time signature: the *allemande* settles into a very sedate and classic four-four: and the *valse* rocks in a three-four feel. As a composer, I was trying to explore the dynamic of duality and triangularity. So — there's *that*.

For the storyteller, every creative piece likely has some autobiographical tendencies and revelations. At the same time, every piece should also be about something outside and beyond oneself: a transcendence that makes one feel small and insignificant; something reaching toward, touching, maybe even lucky enough to embrace, the infinite — the universal. In "Swirling," there is musicality in the natural flow, an organic quality; a feeling in the gentle rhythm of its pulse, its heartbeat, the cadence of Mother Earth, from the whispers of her babbling brooks to the cascading of her raging rivers, to the vast expanses of her oceans and clouds up in the sky.

(*Oh wow, man* — that last sentence runs on like James Joyce on a gummy. Right, then — how's this?)

It's kinda like folkie strumming.

Look, I started writing this stuff while hanging out in a rented *barn*. Then, when I got to my new studio, Eli's Loft, the windows revealed the treetops and skyline in three directions. For the first time in my life, I could be working on music while glancing up to gaze at clouds in motion and branches swaying in the breeze. After five decades in windowless studios, or home basements, this place offered fresh perspectives. Mother Nature was making her presence felt.

The form of "Swirling," in a waltzing six-eight time signature, follows a very logical kind of architecture — two-bar phrases of melody and accompanying chords stack up into four chunks, for eight-bar "A" and "B" sections. (You'll recall I mentioned duality trying to integrate with triangularity.) There's an added four-bar turn at the end of the "B," to bring the key sense back around to where it started (since that "B" section modulates to the key of A voicings, from the swirl of four different key changes in the verse!). The contrasting bridge "C" section settles down into a landscape of E minor and G major, for fourteen bars, which begin with an eight-bar melody, subsequently developed through a new four-bar section. Then the form stretches at the end of twelve bars, adding another two bars to build some energy and tension while also accomplishing a key change to take the listener back to the (originally established) key of D, and the returning "A" section. The melody rides the chord changes and always features chord tones on the downbeats — a straightforwardness that allows the swirl to be felt in the rhythmic, harmonic cadences.

A river is an archetypical metaphor in literature and song, from Al Green to Bruce Springsteen to Garth Brooks to Henry Mancini to Oscar Hammerstein II. (How's *that* for an eclectic country club?) It holds baptismal rebirth because, like life and time, it keeps flowing, conjuring all the elemental potential of water. For dozens of undeniable reasons, water keeps rising up in my creative music writing.

In the case of this piece, the swirling current is about a very human dance, people finding themselves within a moment in time and flowing along with it, adjusting themselves to its momentum. Yet at the same time, the moment should be informed by an awareness of where it leads. The swirling eddies of the running river head to the sea, to the tides, to the evaporation, condensation, and precipitation of the hydrologic water cycle. (A recurring, inspirational kind of underlying creative theme for me. Mother Nature just outside the windows: *outside in, inside out*, and all that.)

From another metaphorical angle, allow me to suggest that every note ever made is just a droplet in the cycles of a musical creative process. To write this out in words makes it seem inaccurately, inappropriately epic in scale (*or maybe that's just a gummy talking*). That's because it's primal, fundamental — just like water, headed downhill, assuming the shape of its container. Water, which is somewhere between 55 and 60 percent of the human body. Water, dancing in six-eight time.

The four "A" verse key changes, in eight bars, reminds me of a precedent: the slippery style of the tune that Steve Morse and I wrote for Triumph's *Surveillance* album, "All the King's Horses." The "B" section, set with altered A voicings up and down the fretboard, switches things up and puts me in mind of a Roger Hodgson, "Give a Little Bit" Supertramp vibe. But his tune wasn't grooving on a *courante*. Still — I do like it when a few chord strums conjure this lyric in my head:

*"See the man with the lonely eyes, oh, take his hand, you'll be surprised . . ."*

An invitation to the dance . . .

Hopefully, the recording and mixing of "Swirling" sounds like it's moving in and out of phase, flowing along on its natural momentum, created by gravitational pull. All this fluttering of fingers, the gentle twisting of wrists — it leads us back inside ourselves: *inside out, outside in.*

— ◆ —

Le courant de la rivière, dirigé vers la mer.

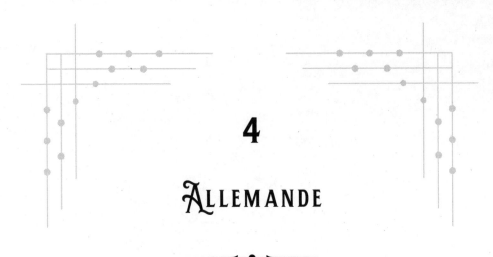

# 4

# ALLEMANDE

———◆———

*You dance love, and you dance joy, and you dance dreams.*

— GENE KELLY

T HERE ARE STORIES WITHIN STORIES WITHIN STORIES.
And so on, and so forth.

The autumn of 2022 found us living temporarily in an Airbnb
nineteenth-century barn conversion while our house underwent
a major reno. A commission arrived, out of the blue, to write
and record an original bourrée for a documentary film.

This got me thinking about the rituals of both informal
and formal dances — how Baroque eighteenth-century court
musicians composed suites, building upon common paired
folk-dance social customs dating back to the 1300s.

We humans — we do like to dance. Jigs and reels, and
square-dancing in the barn, where we *do-si-do* and *allemande*

*left*. From Samoan hakas to Iroquois war dances to intricate Zulu tribal team choreography, we *dance*.

While Jeannette and I patiently waited out the stretch of 2022's winter turning into January 2023, I was writing in the barn by day. In the evenings, we binged *Yellowstone* and its violent soap opera theatre, with its sweeping "God's Country" vibes and atmospheres. Composer Brian Tyler's score demonstrated the dramatic musical possibilities that took the rootsy immigrant styles of Americana, evoking the direct nature of cowboy campfire songs, and amalgamated that with a few strategically placed hoedowns.

While most of my guitar collection had gone into storage for the run of the rental, I'd brought along a Telecaster and a Godin archtop electric — one for downstairs, another for the bedroom loft.

Those circumstances got me scheming about combining a 24.75-inch scale length and Les Paul string profile into a Telly body and neck, creating a hybrid model. I do love my Tellies — but seduced fairly early on by jazz archtops (and in particular one Guild X500 now in residence with the Hard Rock Café organization), I tend to dig in deep with my right hand when playing fingerstyle, which sometimes makes my nails tick and tap annoyingly against the closely-underlying pickguard of a Telly. That's why, for rock gigs, I favoured my solidbody archtop Les Pauls for their neck angle and bridge height, which creates more space between the string plane and the face of the guitar.

This once again raises the sub-theme of *space* — this time in guitar design and human interactions. The spatial design of the guitar accommodates the comfort of my right-hand fingers; the arrangement of the musical piece accommodates the movement of the dance. Both formulations contribute to phrasing that allows for the musical spaces to open and close, widen and narrow.

In this particular composition, I was also (characteristically) hybridizing, channelling cowboy melodies into a little J.S. Bach, some Ernesto Lecuona ("Malaguena"), and a fair bit of Isaac Albéniz (Suite Española, Op. 47). Concurrently, in my poetry writing, I had developed an autofictional protagonist, Alvaro "Alvie" Follis. Alvie is the kind of court jester who can get up on a soapbox, thumb his nose at authority and get away with it. That's because he's well under the radar, so to speak, and officially a clown — a harmless entertainer — akin to rock-star musicians from Canada, known for their self-deprecating and apologetic sense of humour.

Speaking of space — I didn't channel Alvie for this piece, but I did imagine the headspace of a court composer, perhaps a colleague of Alvie's, having to satisfy his patron from the ruling class of nobility, with a solemn work that had a melodic through-line, one that satisfied the "air," the vibe, that a gentle, steady, walking, dance tempo could accommodate.

Mostly, though, when it comes to composing pieces — even with historical alter-ego head spaces — I'm just trying to build constructions that make sense to me as I continue the lifelong search for myself.

Now — I imagine an *allemande* as a historical forerunner of couples' line dancing. In four-four time, it features a stately, courtly kind of energy, at a moderate tempo. You could think of it as a very civilized mating ritual. That's partly what I was doing.

The *allemande* (the term derives from a French name for a Germanic region), spread through European courts four or five centuries ago. By the time it reached Emmett's Telecaster Court, the story was unfolding in four-bar phrases, moving from the tonic to the dominant, leading to a "B" section set in the relative minor key (common to a few of the tales told here).

The formality is reinforced and emphasized by the simplicity, giving the scaling an intentionally deliberate, considerate quality (the "civilized ritual" vibe). After reading my confessions about percolating tendencies in "So Pushy," you might well imagine that the challenge of taming my inner rock star to handle a deliberate, slow-moving ballad is close-to-impossible territory for me. (It is.) I can *hear* it in my head; I can imagine it happening. But to achieve it within the physical technique of my playing is a humbling exercise, in which futility and impatience sumo-wrestle while I'm holding my breath, hoping the combatants (*so pushy*) can just remain in the ring until the match mercifully ends in an exhausted draw.

Despite walk- and hall-of-fame inductions, and a published memoir, I still feel the need to set my "rock star" label in quotes. It undeniably fits, and I tolerate its convenience because I was pretty good at summoning what it took up on stage under a spotlight. Otherwise, however, it generates a lot of misleading hype.

Let's address that.

Back in my Triumph days, I'd put classical guitar pieces on many albums, a facet of my career that I really loved. Oh, it reinforced some critical perceptions of me as an eclectic gadabout, puffing up like a stylistic dilettante too often. But the flip side of that shallow coin is that I was (and still am) an artist who appreciates challenges from a wider range of activities and styles. I love cartoons. I love the cultures of baseball and pro hockey. I love reading and writing from many different quarters. (All reflected in my Instagram feed.) I've always had a sincere appreciation of many styles of music, and my indiscriminating taste doesn't care to recognize and honour any hard borders and boundaries (or ghettoization) of rock, pop, jazz, blues, folk, and classical music. Those guitar pieces I'd written and recorded between 1976 and 1988 created a whole sub-textual alias for my rock star profile, but I'm just a folkie-blues rocker who was always eclectic.

And there I still was, in a rented barn in December of 2022, chasing eighteenth-century classical fingerstyle on an electric guitar and enjoying the struggle.

Some folks might see a "rock star" label and imagine it bestows guitar hero omnipotence. But I'm not even much of a Swiss Army knife, any more than I am a dilettante. These instrumental guitar pieces of mine delve into the colours and vernacular of different styles, but that's just me being me. I'm always looking to stay in the Guitar Club, but never intending to graduate into any exclusive stratum of limited purists or specialists. It's not intended to gain membership into *any* exclusive club of purists or specialists.

The Triumph-recorded guitar pieces were B cuts (more truthfully, C and D cuts) off hard-rock albums over thirteen years, giving our band a one-member-thin veneer of "progressive." In another way, simply because of my own natural inclinations (and "dog's breakfast" influences), some of those pieces sounded like they were inspired by Fernando Sor or Francisco Tarrega in the 1800s. That's more or less how it played to fans who were paying attention. To most other folks in the wider world, who only caught wind of reputation and gossip from a distance, that breeze left its own impressions. That's how showbiz PR often blows, in my experience.

Anyway — here we are in 2023, where "Allemande" is really not much different in style and execution than my "Petite Etude" of '81 or "A Minor Prelude" of '82. Maybe it's a bit slower — a bit more mature, mellowed — a bit more seasoned, in terms of the composer and performing artist. Maybe forty years has taught me a thing or two about this kind of playing.

Maybe not.

> *Does my song ring true? You get to decide*
> *or is it just another chapter in the Big Big Lie?*
>
> — RIK EMMETT, "BIG LIE," *Absolutely* ALBUM (1990)

"Allemande" (and "Winter Nocturne," which concludes the tales) have layers that concern themselves with the notions of space. Claude Debussy famously claimed that music is not so much about the notes, but the spaces between them. Updating the notion, Miles Davis said, "It's not the notes you play — it's the notes you don't play." In my music making, I keep trying to take that heady concept to heart — then transmit the restraint to my hands (which sometimes run on motor memory, with minds of their own).

The "Allemande" verse did not feel entirely satisfying until I placed the IV minor (Fm9) in the back half of bar six in the "B" section. This gave the whole thing a destination, and the creative construction began to make sense to me as the surrounding architecture was leading to that spot-lit location. I knew I was finally on to something. Nevertheless, the piece still didn't feel complete — until I came up with a "middle 8" bridge (the "C" section), which became the last quadrant of the puzzle completed.

*Speaking of bridges:* a very common methodology of song-writers is that the composition of a bridge section arrives, not as an afterthought, but more like the *last* thought: the contrasting, slight vacation from the atmosphere of the tune, that gives the creative piece an overall balance and satisfying payoff of form. Many of the ten tales feature bridges, mostly because I find they satisfy my sense of a song's wholeness or completion. A bridge is a metaphor — connecting different perspectives and offering itself as a way to get out of a place, while at the same time providing the way back home.

I think the world can always use more songs that have great bridges. They are a story within a story within a story: and so on, and so forth.

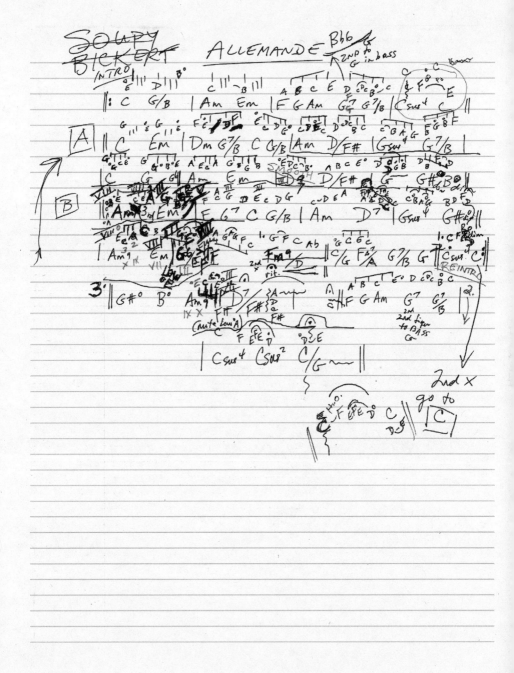

133

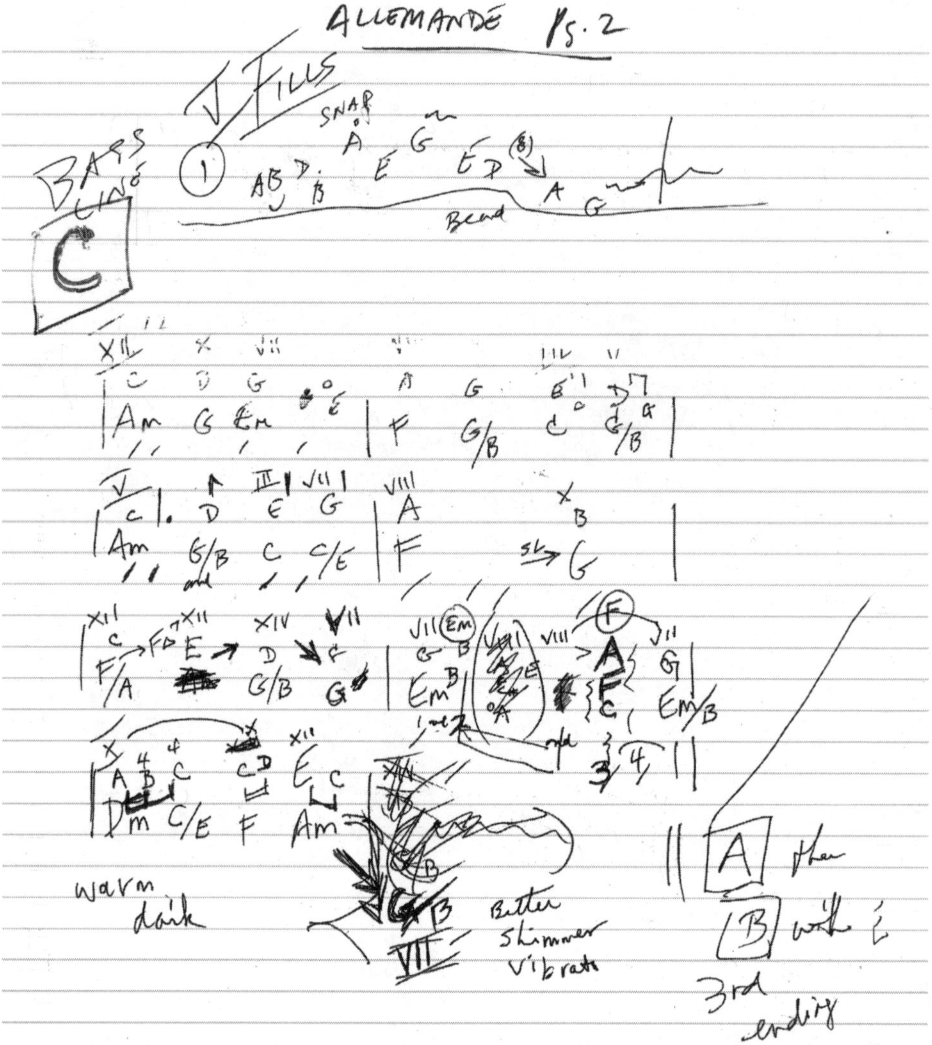
ALLEMANDE Pg. 2
FILLS
BASS LINE
SNAP
Bend
warm
dark
Better
Shimmer
Vibrato
A then
B with
3rd
ending

# 5

# COWBOY AND
# GAUCHO WALTZ

## (VALSE A RASGUEADO)

————◄●►————

*So you find yourself on this rock, spinning round the sun*
*Where the clock hands colour every chance*
*Before the music's over and your songs have all been sung*
*Tell me — what will you bring to the dance?*

— RIK EMMETT, "THE LONGING," *The Spiral Notebook* ALBUM (1995)

TANDARD FIRST-POSITION GUITAR CHORDS ARE ONE OF
the most aesthetic pleasures that the instrument has to
offer. Nicknamed "cowboy chords," a handful of them opens
the floodgates toward dozens of simple folk songs, for evenings
around the campfire. That basic accessibility of a guitar sets this
waltz on its journey, picking through a few chords in a rhythm
that conjures the paces of a cantering horse, the sweep of an
open skyline — the romance of a high-plains drifter, a loner
up in the saddle, listening to the melodies forming in his head,

emerging later to work themselves out before the campfire. (Like I said — we were watching a lot of *Yellowstone*.)

Here in the cowboy's waltz, the melodic composition tries to establish a bit of a prevailing wind at his back.

Then, the chorus leads him down through the southwest, as gringo cowboys turn into gauchos and the chord landscape shifts the heritage from Appalachian to Andalusian.

Yet the rhythm is constant — a universal appeal compelling enough to span centuries. In this humble instance, the heart and soul of the *valse* suggested a little cowboy swing tune, with a hummable chorus. Later on, the mood evolves with the harmonic atmosphere, morphing into the rasgueado of the Romani.

This storyteller's canon shares a strong link to "El Cuento Del Gadjo" from the *Ten Invitations* project of 1997, feeding the sub-theme layer of how the tales owe so much to other narratives from my past. This particular Spanish/Romani/Arabic strain goes as far back on record as 1978's "El Duende Agonizante."

Analyzing the nuts and bolts of the construction reveals the campfire strumming of the intro leading into an eight-bar "A" verse section, establishing a straightforward folk melody. This sets up an eight-bar "B" section (the cowboy chorus), over a progression of four chords that so many pop songs use — I V VIm IV — which, hopefully, lends the moment an accessible kind of comfort.

This section gets an elastic stretch of some extra bars at its end. In songwriting workshops, I used to call this particular method of unbalancing a form "pulling the taffy"— generating a building tension with its subsequent sweet, welcome release.

After a re-intro, the whole construction repeats.

Then a new "C" section comes along, ratcheting up the rasgueado factor, functioning (unsurprisingly, for me) like a bridge, before a return to the chorus for the (hopefully familiar and satisfying) third time. But I'd also come up with an aggressive extra riff, a new chord progression where the movement shifted to a chromatic descension in the bass. I decided to use it as a "D" section — a coda — upping the ante with an accented rhythmic variation, raising the dynamic energy until the intentional drama of a final decrescendo/crescendo signals the arrival of its four-bar conclusion.

◂ ◦ ▸

This "Barn Dance Suite" began with the polite phasing swirl of the courante. The insistence of the valse, with its vigorous energy and an intense churning of flamenco skirts, makes the gaucho's strumming the obvious climax for the proceedings.

The caballero might display a bit more unbridled emotion than the folkie cowboy, but they've established a common ground, strumming their guitars in the firelight.

*What will you bring to the dance?*

In 2023, in one of my tales, it's not *what*, but *who*.

I brought a cowboy and a gaucho, waltzing around the campsite.

Cowboy Pg. 2

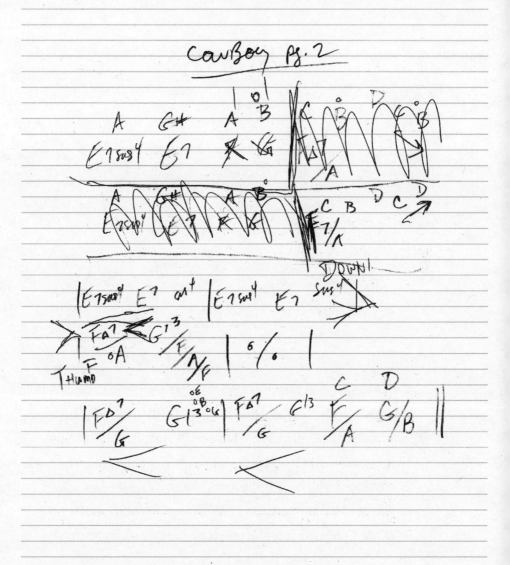

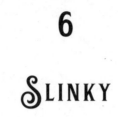

# 6

# SLINKY

◂ ● ▸

*You're my spark of nature's fire*
*You're my sweet, complete desire*
*Sunny, one so true — I love you*

— BOBBY HEBB, "SUNNY," *Sunny* ALBUM (1966)

IN APRIL OF THE YEAR THAT I FINISHED GRADE 8, Bobby Hebb released his classic R&B track entitled "Sunny." Set in a minor key, it has a really smooth progression that eventually leads to the V dominant 7 chord, before the proceedings arrive back at the lyric "I love you" on the I minor.

"Sunny" led to the Classics IV's song "Spooky," which I remember from my youth in 1968. I perceived a connectivity.

*Love is kinda crazy with a spooky little girl like you.*

— BUDDY BUIE, HARRY MIDDLEBROOKS JR., JAMES B. COBB JR., MIKE SHAPIRO

"Spooky" was remade by the Atlanta Rhythm Section in 1979, becoming a hit all over again.

And speaking of kinships, the Classics IV followed "Spooky" up with a similarly-styled song, "Stormy," within the very same year.

All of this serves as background to the fact that as soon as I started jamming with myself on the II—V, the Em7 to A7 chord change, a song germinating in my noggin, I knew it would need a title to fall within the tradition. (Plus, beats one and three of the tempo seemed to establish the bobbing pace of one of those coil-wired Slinky toys flipping over itself while descending a staircase.)

By the way — early noodling on this happened through an Electro-Harmonix K9 pedal, via its Fender Rhodes electric piano tremolo patch, which helped me discover the atmospheric vibe of this piece. While I knew it would have to feature something similar to that effect, the K9 pedal had too much lo-fi extraneous noise for me. I thought I could chase something via plug-ins later in the game (that part of the story is addressed in detail in the addenda).

As this "Slinky" piece was developing, I kept telling myself not to overthink it — just let it flow naturally, moving in an unhurried, sexy, R&B way. A few licks seemed to benefit from popping and snapping the strings, like a funk bass player. Working Babs with my right-hand fingers the way Jeff Beck worked his Strats, I summoned other (name-dropping) influences: a little bit of Stevie Ray Vaughan attitude, married to some simplified George Benson, Kenny Burrell, and a bit of Grant Green thrown in for good measure.

*This is what I often do:*
*"Slinky" is a gumbo stew.*

In keeping with one of the sub-themes of this project, I plundered the old catalogue for new spins on ideas that came from my conceptual wheelhouse, liberally cribbing from my recent playbook. If a listener is familiar with the sequences and chord cycles of "Step Ladder" and "Kosmic Tricycle" from *The Bonfire Sessions* (2020), they'd hear some seasoned chunks of that cooking away in here.

From experience, I know that this will be the kind of guitar piece I can take liberties with over the years as it becomes more familiar. For example — the fills in between the vamping head chord changes can be improvised, every time. But when I kept experimenting and improvising different licks while rehearsing "Slinky" in pre-production, the consistency of my performance suffered. I then decided to establish three licks and stick to repeating them the three times they occur in the arrangement of this recording. (Three is often the magic number of music construction. It favours memorability and accessibility.) By limiting my ad lib choices, I enhanced my ability to memorize and solidify the content, and capture a higher-quality take.

Those with sharp ears might hear that the turnaround Fmaj7 lick in bar five of the "B" section is the same little chord lick used in the third verse of "So Pushy." Not only that, the chord progression in that same "B" section bridge from bars nine to twelve is the same chord progression that happens in bars nine to twelve of the "B" section of "The Rio Glide." These are not the only self-referential quotes that happen in the ten songs: this was a deliberate layer when composing the tales. Not only was I borrowing from my own older catalogue, I was also creating subtle infrastructure and linking the pieces together by having them quote little bits of each other. (Steal from yourself and they'll call it your *style*!)

This track contains ingredients that work for me sonically — a lot of short little glissando slides *up*, often on the bass note of a chord, contrasted by some strategic placements of slide-offs *down* the sixth string, an expressive ornament my pal Mike Shotton refers to as a *"voo."* Whenever the four-chords-in-one-bar sequence happens, which leads into the "A" or "B" section, the first chord needs to have the bass note slide up and into position — just as beat four of the last bar of the "B" section bridge needs to be a nice solid *voo* sliding down, to set up the re-intro. (*Slides* are *"slinky."*) These kinds of guitarisms are like punctuation — a dash to start a clause, or an exclamation mark at the end of a sentence. If a guitarist can be described as "talking" on the instrument, it's these kinds of things that add a lot of expression to it. (Musicians who have worked with me know that my shortcut to communicating music often uses scat language: nonsense words and phrases that improvise consonants and vowels, mimicking where I might be hearing hard, loud notes or softer, rounder tones. Sometimes, when working out melodic guitar parts, I find it helpful to "scat" them, in order to find the natural flow of tone, attack, rhythm, and colour that I want the notes to have.)

Anyone familiar with the arts and crafts of recording knows that one of its surprising joys is the happy accident. On the afternoon of December 6, we were mixing this "Slinky" track. From my yack-yack about the sound of a Fender Rhodes electric piano, Blair knew I was imagining the sound of stereo tremolo — an intentional randomizing effect that alters one's perception of the notes, making it more about the sensual experience of the sound, as opposed to just the notes that make up the music. I'd gone down out of Eli's Loft to the kitchen, to make us a bit of lunch. Searching through some unfamiliar plug-ins on his computer, Blair stumbled across a Native Instruments effect called the FREAK, in Oscillator mode. He called out — said he wasn't sure, but maybe he'd found something great, and didn't want to touch or adjust anything until I heard it.

It was perfect — exactly what I'd been hearing in my head. There it was, now — floating in the air.

Gotta *love* happy accidents.

———•———

*Accidentally on purpose.*

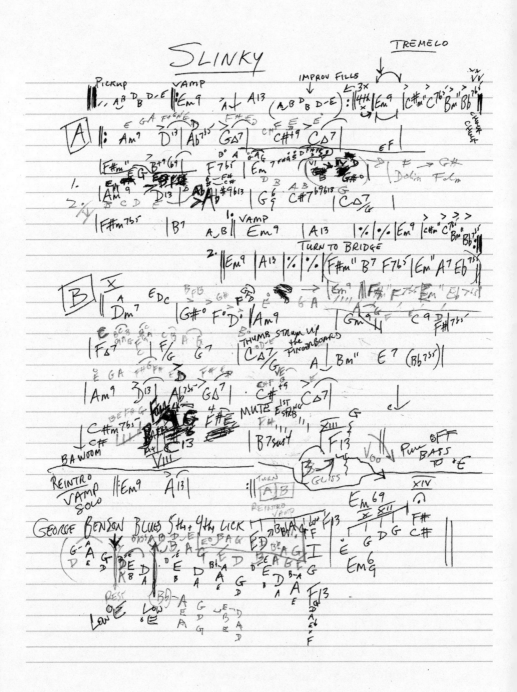

# 7

# BURLYTOWN

──◆●▶──

*Reggae music is a music of integrity; reggae's consciousness was built on a message. My music speaks of love, equality and spirituality, and I would hope that one finds this integrity in my music.*

— STEPHEN MARLEY

IN DISCUSSING THE SONG "SO PUSHY" EARLIER, I QUOTED James Baldwin. In that tune, I was acknowledging my teenage history, learning blues licks.

Then I went on to have a lifelong career. One of the ironies in experiencing varying stages of commercial success is that some folks only know and care about the "you" from the time period that contributed something to the soundtrack of their own lives — *their* history. My wife, Jeannette, would scoff at something like this and say, "Not such a heavy cross to bear, Rocket."

That soundtrack helped to provide the sustenance of my lifelong pursuits, and those evergreen songs have become a series of lodestones. They have to be acknowledged and considered from time to time, simply because that's the reality of the obligations in an oh-so-public career.

Artists from Picasso to Stravinsky to T.S. Eliot have acknowledged that stealing is a necessary component of creativity. I've also been led to understand that stealing from yourself is an expression of style.

In this particular case, "Burlytown" owes a healthy portion of its DNA to the lodestone "Fight the Good Fight," from Triumph's *Allied Forces* album (1981).

Stephen Marley's quote, above, speaks of a conscientious loyalty to integrity in music. I've always liked the idea that music can carry some kind of message — or messages — within it. Although I'm not a reggae artist, by any stretch, after the successful evergreen integrities of "Fight," the vibe of a reggae feel has sometimes returned to inform my writing: "Never Surrender," "Raise High," and "The Miracle of Love" made it to records. The compelling tendency of that feel gives a song more of a strut in the way that it moves. Its message has an inherent blend of the corporeal with the spiritual.

Cast your mind back to Tina Turner, in the video for "What's Love Got to Do with It," hitting her stride when the chorus drops. That perambulation transcends time and space. As soon as I got a bit of a chord progression going for the verse of "Burlytown," I had mental images of Tina walking the walk.

Now, I particularly enjoy when the character written into a piece marries nicely with both the tone of a particular guitar and the audio sound of an applied guitar effect — for example, Chris Stapleton's guitar sound on "Tennessee Whiskey." I can't imagine any other guitar sound being right for that song, that groove, that feel, that vibe. It's perfection. Likewise, B.B. King on "The Thrill Is Gone." Or the twin guitar tones of Don Felder and Joe Walsh on the solo of "Hotel California" (set over Felder's capoed twelve-string guitar). These aren't just classics because they're unforgettable songs; the recordings have a character that the *sound* of those guitars enhances perfectly. They could certainly be done differently, but couldn't be captured any better.

There are dozens of other examples that have heavily influenced my music making. In that list would be Jimmy Page's solo on "Stairway to Heaven"; Jeff Beck's on "Cause We've Ended as Lovers"; and Roy Buchanan's on "The Messiah Will Come Again." (Examples chosen because they all went down via Telecaster guitars.)

The thing is — I'm also the kind of guitarist with inspirations from all over the map. I could just as easily refer to "Li'l Darlin'" by Joe Pass as one of my favourite examples of a perfect guitar tone. Flatwound strings on a Gibson 175 archtop, played fingerstyle, is a tone for the ages. Ditto, George Benson's floating ad-lib cadenzas at the beginning of "Affirmation" from *Breezin'*. Or Julian Bream on nylon string classical guitar, playing *Granados & Albéniz* in a rich, long reverb.

———•———

*Sweet dreams are made of this.*

For my ten tales, sonically, the Joni Mitchell masterpiece *Hejira* got me going. Something started there, between her and engineer Henry Lewy, that I wanted to explore in my own twenty-first-century digital way. That thinking eventually mutated like wildfire throughout the recordings of the Ten Telecaster Tales. As I practised and rehearsed throughout pre-production, my Roland Cube 80 amp got a full workout on the EFX knob that offers chorus, phaser, flanger, and tremolo. Once I started recording demos in Pro Tools with Steve Skingley as my engineer, later capturing mixes with my friend Blair Packham, I eschewed the Roland EFX in the amp and committed to chasing more dramatic flavours via plug-ins.

Blair and I didn't have to work too hard to find a sonic pocket for "Burlytown." (That makes it sound like I was sharing the workload, but Blair did all the driving, and I was more like a bossy consultant, navigating from the copilot seat.) The verses sit in a subtle stereo chorus effect, and when the choruses hit, the rotating Leslie simulator kicks in. One of my favourite sonic moments in the tales happens when the bridge arrives in this song and the reverb opens up as a velvety backspace. That's goosebump territory.

If I had it to do again, I would switch to thicker, higher gauge strings on Babs for this track (as well as "Allemande" and "The Rio Glide" — maybe "Cowboy and Gaucho Waltz," too). In particular, you can hear a too-skinny tone when I pick hard on the last single-note run down at 3:12. I wish the guitar had been fighting me back a little harder for that. But that's the way it went down that day, and it is what it is.

Now, I like a story rooted in a strong sense of place. Beyond the walls of Eli's Loft, my Burlytown is a place where I find that the groove never rests. In a waterfront boardwalk town, the south shore lights twinkle across the wave action of the bay after sunsets. But it's also a city that boasts of a mighty bridge — literally called The Skyway, across the western end of Lake Ontario. The last of the Great Lakes defines the downtown's southern limit, adorned with a beautiful pier and a lakefront park that hosts a large number of events throughout the year. It's a music town, full of the military rudiments of marching bands, country pickers, symphony orchestra players, jazzers, and buskers. Every summer, the Sound of Music Festival brings rock 'n' roll to the city core. (Memorably, my rock band was invited to play the event in the summer of 2015: I then performed as a guest artist with the Burlington Symphony Orchestra in Spencer Smith Park on Canada Day, 2017.)

My pal Mike Shotton has his studio, The Underground, up the line from me, where I have spent many enjoyable hours chasing after sounds and turning them into digital ones and zeroes (which is the more modern version of a game I used to play back in the last century, turning ideas into magnetic particles on tape).

In "Burlytown," the melodic phrases of the verse and chorus each follow the same pattern of a one-bar "call" melody with a one-bar "response." The verses are set in E minor, and the choruses shift up into the relative G major. There's a simplicity to this that appeals to me: melodic writing that features a kind of back and forth, a counter-offer, balancing the flow.

Intentionally, the bridge conjures up the ghost of a chord progression idea I'd also employed forty-three years ago in "Fight the Good Fight" — except here, for "Burlytown," it's been moved up a tone to E minor and features more inversions, stretching and heading upwards, using the whole length of the fingerboard to give it a dramatically enhanced melodic range and construction (no vocals or lyric, after all).

The work inside the reggae-fied groove carries a fair bit of tension — dramatic shifts of dynamics, a veiled threat of menacing power; then sudden bursts of bright colours, with the choruses arriving as celebrations, followed by the abrupt imposition of right-hand edge-of-palm damping. Yet the unrelenting pulse of the groove maintains a backbeat rhythm that never quits.

That strength of character made me indulge in the wordplay of Burlington as "burly." For me, the potential of my fictional Burlytown is wide open: its groove does not discriminate. The beauty of its unique exclusivity is that (of all things) it is so *inclusive* — just one of the many enigmatic mysteries of music.

> *Music gives a soul to the universe, wings to the mind, flight to the imagination, and life to everything.*
>
> — PLATO

Yeah. I think Plato would've dug a reggae groove.

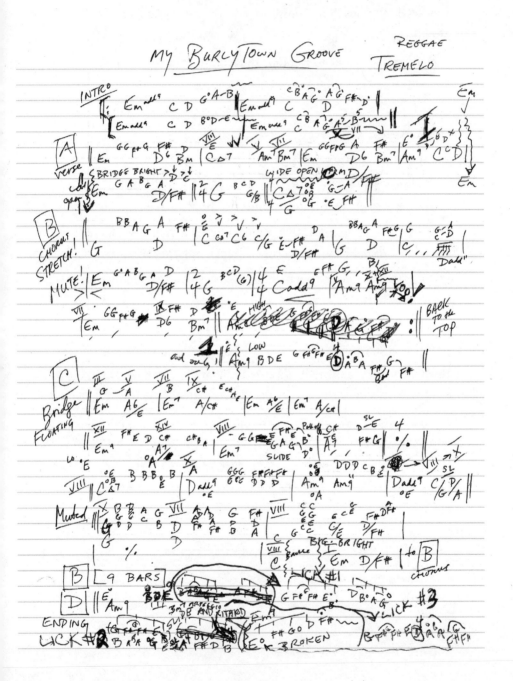

# MY BURLYTOWN GROOVE

REGGAE
TREMELO

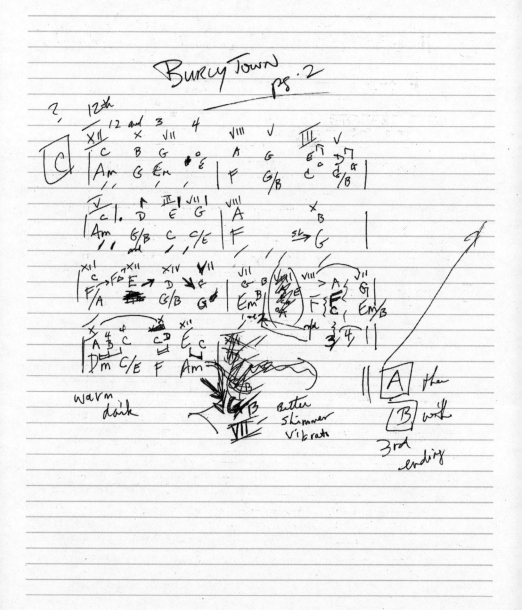

Burly Town pg. 2

# 8

# THE RIO GLIDE

◄—●—►

I N THE SPRING OF 1973, AT NINETEEN YEARS YOUNG,
I auditioned for the Humber College music program's guitar
department head, Peter Harris. One of the audition pieces I chose
was "Girl from Ipanema" because I'd recently caught Charlie
Byrd performing live at the Colonial Tavern on Yonge Street in
Toronto, where his nylon-string finger stylings spoke worlds to me.

Fashioning his playing style after Lenny Breau, Harris was
quite adept at Kenny Dorham's "Blue Bossa," and Peter would
become one of my mentors.

I've always tried to emulate the way he handled the vibe
of music like this. The samba and the bossa nova required the
fluidity of an ultra-smooth control. The rhythms have something in the way they move. Hips that sway, curves that shift,
just *so* — the intimacy of a solo guitar is perfectly suited for the
ambulation of this style.

I've always taken side trips into both classical and jazz guitar stylings. As a lifelong music lover, I'm attracted to Latin grooves with a deep respect. The ambitions of jazz musicians often lead them to command certain styles — in particular the syncopation of swing, Latin, funk, and rhythm and blues. I would certainly never claim mastery of anything. But with these Telecaster Tales, I wanted to challenge myself to explore wider and go deeper into ranges of solo stylistic expression than I had before.

A bossa nova lays bare the limitations of my technique and craft. I admit, it's hard to keep the bass notes controlled, even and smooth. But the artistic question to face in my eighth decade of life is — if I'm not going to give it a go now — *when?*

As I recorded the material in Eli's Loft with Blair engineering, a running gag between us became the invocation of the name *Glenn Gould*. (Mostly after my little clams and weird artifacts of lousy technique scarred and littered the takes, requiring surgical, digital editing of the material.) The irony of our joking arose from the stories I'd heard from both Ed Stone and Hugh Cooper (beloved house engineers at Triumph's Metalworks Studios back in the heyday). Before their MW tenure, they were employed out of the Sounds Interchange studio and had been hired to work on remote sessions with Glenn Gould on grand pianos in rented hotel ballrooms, where very intense editing was a routine of Gould's approach, as he meticulously used his recording process to perfect what would become the finished product he offered to the public. Gould used the tools of the trade to work at the highest of major-league levels. Me? I use 'em to grasp at some of the midrange rungs of the recording business ladder — and hold on for dear life.

*(There's no doubt Gould was prescient about where recording technology could and did lead. And there will be more discussion about this later in the book, at the tail end of the "Winter Nocturne" chapter, when I discuss David Byrne's take on present technology, and what it might mean for our future. But for now, back to "The Rio Glide.")*

When I would listen back to takes of it, I was reminded of the advice that Chet Atkins offered, both in interviews and in his own stylish performances. He counselled that fancy-pants virtuosic challenges are *beside* the much more important point of always being smooth and making the part you play sit with a beautiful feel.

*Feel* is everything.

And that has always remained a strong challenge for me — trying to harness my eager enthusiasm and find ways to let the music itself lead me. A big lesson I learned from taking on the Ten Telecaster Tales was one of patience, acceptance of limits, and trying to let the feel of my rhythms lead every facet of the proceedings. And I relearned the lesson that there will *always* be a lot more to learn because one of the truths of music is its infinite nature.

I felt a strong inclination to insert an extra "A" and "B" verse into this arrangement, because it felt like the piece should function like a standard, heading off into improvised variations that depart from the melody, as jazz tunes so often do. I decided against it because I would have had to create a bed track of chord comping, for blowing lead guitar over top, and

I wanted to stick to the original concept — solo guitar. I also rationalized that the smooth, relaxed nature of this tune had already been established by simply stating the melody over top of the changes, and at this stage of its young life, my modest little tune had hardly become a jazz standard built for blowing. As a tune, it felt complete (enough). As a Beatle once advised, channelling his mother Mary, "Let It Be." So I stuck to a basic singer-songwriter instinct.

During mixing, looking for a slightly higher aesthetic level, I asked myself (and challenged Blair), what might the heat waves, filtering the visuals on a Rio beach, *sound* like? Could we get some *shimmer* of glistening skin, *shimmering* through the heat waves, as something worth watching *shimmies* down the strand?

What does the air sound like when one is gliding along?

Let's head to the beach and saunter on down the board-walk, paying our respects to Antônio Carlos Jobim . . . and the resonances of Peter Harris and Charlie Byrd.

I hope you folks can hear how warm and calm it is.

I hope you can feel some of my gratitude.

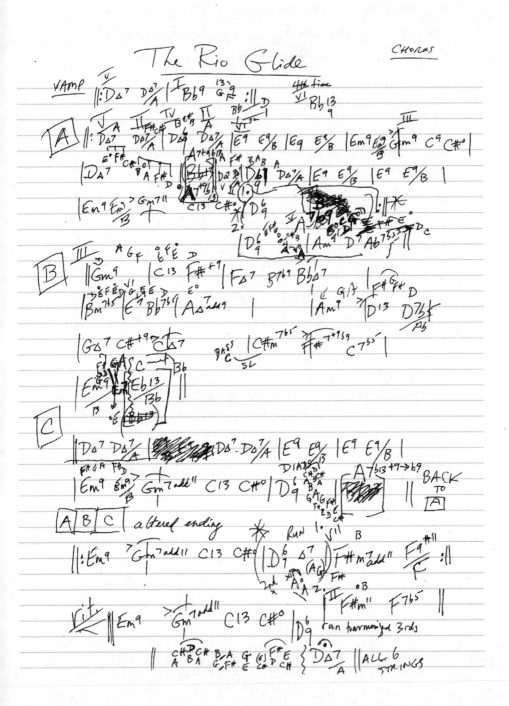

The Rio Glide

158

# 9

# GEE WHIZ

*Everybody's always afraid of being considered old-fashioned,*
*but I'm not. I don't give a damn. I like that fat sound of the*
*rhythm section and I use it to put down a feeling of cooking.*

— MARTY GROSZ, JAZZ JOURNAL INTERNATIONAL, NOVEMBER 1992

ONE OF MY PERSONAL MUSICAL TRADITIONS BEGAN ON the album *Ipso Facto*, with the walking-bass/chord progression song, "Woke Up This Morning." "Taste of Steel" and "Mr. Bebop" on *Swing Shift* followed; then "Beacon Street Hotel" on *Good Faith* and "Little Ditty" on *Marco's Secret Songbook*. "Blue Sky Train" and "Takes All Kinds" continued the run on *The Bonfire Sessions*.

Now "Gee Whiz" has become the latest contribution to the tradition, and cribs from the lot.

Set in the standard guitar blues jam key of G, this piece was designed to travel all over the fingerboard, walking around with a bit of chromatic movement in the bass, inside a twelve-bar "A" section that leads to dozens of chords in eight-bar "B" section verses.

As Mr. Grosz might have it, a *fat* rhythm with a *feeling of cooking.*

In a way, this piece combines a lot of other aspects of motion from other tales. Yes, this one has a walking-bass line, but it also definitely struts, slinks, pushes, scratches, swirls, slides, zooms, and swooshes . . . It gets busy. Admittedly, there's a lot of sneaky show-off stuff in this. For that, I'll finger-point at Joe Pass and Chet Atkins for their influence. (Mostly Pass. I will always maintain that Joseph Anthony Jacobi Passalacqua was one of the greatest guitarists who ever graced this planet.)

*Gee whiz.*

Pass and Atkins — sure. *Obviously.* But none of my "fat" jazz cooking would have happened if it hadn't been for Marty Grosz, born in Berlin in 1930.

You can find some of his delightful novelty stuff online — check out "Take Me to the Land of Jazz" on NPR and "When I Take My Sugar to Tea" or "Swing That Music" on YouTube. In an all-star jazz concert billed as The Great Guitars at Roy Thomson Hall in Toronto, I heard Grosz play a song called "I've Got a Chord for Every Note I Sing," and I was hooked. His bloodline reaches back to Dixieland ragtime and hot jazz, and something in it speaks to me and *moves* me.

*Gee whiz.*

No question, I'm a rock 'n' roll guy, mostly self-taught, in terms of technique. But a lot of musical things come down to how your body incorporates the groove of the feel — and I do like to swing.

Plus, I think an innate ability to swing is one of the things that makes other musicians accept your musicality. A perfect example is Led Zeppelin's drummer, John Bonham. Even in his rock grooves, you can sense that he feels the swing in whatever he's laying down. Feel becomes readily apparent when a player easily finds the comfortable pocket of a swinging groove. And this liquid flow of music is also apparent in great singers like Frank Sinatra, Mel Tormé, and Michael Bublé.

I believe it may be possible to teach anyone anything. At least, I believe it enough to give it a shot, in good faith. (I also believe that some of us are lacking in our ranges of potential, and I want to apologize to anyone who ever tried to teach me mathematics, physics, or chemistry — or how to read music notation — because I truly sucked at them all.)

At the same time, I also believe that some folks are born with innate gifts, and I believe I was blessed with modest amounts of some other stuff. One of them is my propensity to swing: to play over a blues shuffle, walk a dotted-eighth/sixteenth line, and make something *happen*.

That groove kicks into motion and my body goes . . .
*Gee whiz.*

162

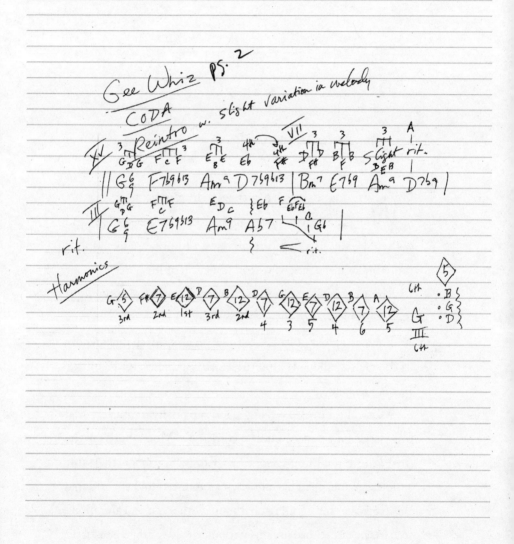

Gee Whiz pg. 2

CODA

163

# 10

# WINTER NOCTURNE

——◄●►——

**W**E'RE COMING TO THE END OF THE STORY CYCLE. The leaves have fallen from the trees, died, and withered away. The world reminds us of how we are simply a finite biological element within the cycle of life.

The progression descends, mentally conjuring moonlight on a fresh blanket of silver-white snow.

There is a great peaceful solitude, yet also a deep melancholy, in the melody that sits atop these drifting flakes. It's beautiful. But it's *cold*.

Musically, I'm also circling back personally to the very first fingerstyle guitar piece I ever recorded — "Moonchild," on the first Triumph album. Also set in Em, using much the same simple, ringing, open harmonics, it announced to the world that this particular rock guitarist harboured other musical ambitions, too. In the end, those dreams gave me a wider range of artistic, creative expression than the bigger rock-star door-crashers provided. (Still — huge gratitude felt and offered up for the fact that both things survived into the third act of my life.)

I do not place any significant personal beliefs in supernatural things. But, from a poetic and romantic perspective (and as the newspaper horoscopes say — *purely for entertainment value*) let's look into something.

I was born on July 10, 1953, at 11:05 p.m., which makes me, astrologically speaking, a Cancer. The moon is the ruling celestial body of Cancerians. In the traditions of astrology, this sign is northern (and I am Canadian, by golly) and, in terms of its elemental categorizing, it's a water sign (from the earth, air, fire and water quartet). The water connection purportedly leads to a negative polarity, with key-word associations like emotion, empathy, and sensitivity. I'm not saying that I put any faith into this kind of horoscope stuff; but, as an artist, I'm happy to draw inspirational subtext from wherever I can find it. And if a Technicolor Dreamcoat does seem to fit, I'll wear it (especially if it lends the tale some plausible secondary belief.)

"Winter Nocturne" is about cycles coming to a moonlit, snow-covered end. The idea of a Telecaster guitar arpeggiating beams of silver-blue moonlight feels right to me, way down deep in my guts. It seems fitting that the echoes fade off into a plug-in called *DreamVerb*. Those musical notes in that order, sitting in those deep, rich effects, feel natural. The water has become crystallized.

The storybook may not have arrived at "happily ever after," but the final note of the piece closes the book. The echoes into reverb shut down, and the sound — suddenly dry — feels right and true.

Now — let me tell you a story of stories within stories. In the history of this world, and the story of this universe, this story here is a sub-atomic particle in a grain of sand on a beach. But it's my truth.

My father passed away on February 12, 2021. I remain haunted by his long, horrible run of degenerating Alzheimer's and escalating cancer, culminating in a lonely, drawn-out passing in a COVID-quarantined retirement facility where we were only allowed to visit one guest at a time, behind plastic face guards that baffled both him and I, in multiple ways. It's been over three years as of this writing, but he still visits me occasionally in my dreams, lingering around while my own aging and decaying mind and body are (obviously) still processing the trauma that's a part of everyone's life, if you live long enough. He was the last of my nuclear family to go; my mom and my two brothers had already left this world. That loss brings to mind so many other losses in my life — and what's a musician to do?

Make music, to come up with *something* that might make sense of the insensate. The music of "Winter Nocturne" is about trying to work out grief, about missing my family, about how the making of music is as ephemeral and short-lived as our lives, circling the sun on this little blue ball.

*Row, row, row your boat / Gently down the stream*
*Merrily, merrily, merrily, merrily / Life is but a dream*

So that's one of the layers in this piece of music. A listener might never arrive at a literal understanding of it, but it's enough if they can sense a feeling of loss, of melancholy mourning, which is a result of the stories within the stories.

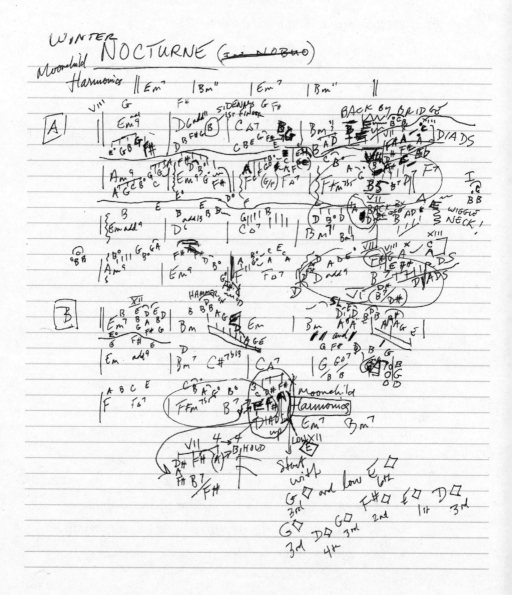

It's not like I wanted to end the Tales on a downer. It was more like, after all of this storytelling, "happily ever after" had evolved into "naturally, ever after." This ending felt more realistic. More righteous. This ending made the most sense.

In his comprehensive book *How Music Works*, David Byrne has a chapter entitled "Technology Shapes Music." There's a short section at the end, tellingly delineated as "That Which Cannot Be Preserved."

As he's teeing up his main point, he writes: "I find music somewhat intrusive in restaurants and bars. Maybe due to my involvement with it, I feel I have to either listen intently or tune it out. Mostly I tune it out . . ."

I envy Mr. Byrne his ability to *mostly* do that. *Mostly*, I can't. The way my brain is wired, even the slightest hint of music immediately becomes the thing *demanding* my attention. I will disregard conversation at any moment (often pissing off the folks around me). It's entirely possible that I could get distracted, floating on air, then absent-mindedly step out into the path of an oncoming bus.

For me, it's more of an all-or-nothing thing — it's not somewhat intrusive. It's a bully. It makes me squirm in obsessive-compulsive inner warfare. I must surrender, or I must suffer the incessant tyranny of the siege.

On the other hand, music fills me up. It completes me. I can surrender to it and become one with the flow of whatever emotions and thoughts that music has to offer.

That's just me.

Anyway — Byrne goes on to elaborate on what technology has been doing to music:

> For me, music is becoming dematerialized, a state that is more truthful to its nature, I suspect. Music technology . . . in some ways appears to have been on a trajectory in which the end result is that it will destroy and devalue itself. It will succeed completely when it self-destructs. The technology is useful and convenient, but it has, in the end, reduced its own value and increased the value of the things it has never been able to capture or reproduce. Technology has altered the way music sounds, how it's composed, and how we experience it. It has also flooded the world with music. . . . playing, hearing and experiencing [music] was exceptional, a rare and special experience. Now hearing it is ubiquitous, and silence is the rarity that we pay for and savor.

David Byrne's observations are provocative, true, and profound — particularly here, as I come to the end of my reasoning and rationalizing about the tales, and specifically, the moods that pervade the recorded track of "Winter Nocturne."

There's no doubt whatsoever in my mind that "serious" music, which is to say — music made for *music's* sake, is on an endangered list, simply because technology has made it far too easy to make music that's intended as wallpaper or a soundtrack or a background-added value to selling other stuff. Artificial Intelligence has consequences that we can't fathom, yet.

I don't think most pop stars set out to become great musicians anymore. They seek to become brands so that they can diversify into various showbiz roles, becoming wealthy and powerful influencers. None of that strikes me as healthy for the future of music getting made for *music's* sake.

Byrne suspects that music's nature is more "truthful" when dematerialized from its technology. Yet music's technology is the very heart (and soul?) of its business — something I've struggled with all my life and, certainly, struggled harder with, after music became both my avocation and vocation.

My ambivalence toward technology (and yet my unavoidable embrace of it) is yet another unavoidable sub-theme — another layer — in the Telecaster Tales.

Yes — there is a purity, a truth, to live performances of music, floating in thin air. In that immediacy, it has unrivalled magic, and any other audio experience fails to capture, possess, and deliver that particular quality of enchantment. This has always been my life experience. The social function of live music performance has its own powerful authenticity, one that no technology can deliver.

Yet technology aids, abets, and enhances music performance.

I originally conceived the music of the Telecaster Tales as a live off-the-floor recording project, capturing a moment in time, one in which technology would be sublimated, so it would not rear its pervasive head.

But my seventy-year-old skill set came up against the wisdom and experience of life as a recording artist, and technology offered me *solutions*.

I blinked, waffled in my ambivalence, then caved.

Can technology not deliver its own kind of truth? Is it possible that it could even be *more* truthful, in different kinds of ways? Truthful to the heart and soul of the music composition itself? Truthful to the bridges being constructed from performer to audience? Truthful to the medium of recording arts and crafts? There's the truth of an unfiltered recording with every miscue and unfortunate performance slip. And then, there's another truth, that chases the integrity of the composition's intent. In 2023, hasn't technology become an absolutely necessary and vital component in the cooking of all the layers I was looking to integrate into the ten tales?

Certainly, my ambivalence toward technology is founded on some solid legitimacy. Because — similar to David Byrne (but not quite at his levels of success) — my own career blundered along. I sought gigs. Then I sought a supplemental side hustle, of making recordings, selling them, getting them airplay.

Ahh, the long and checkered history of technology's mechanical delivery of music. Corporate conglomerates manufacturing hardware and software have always been like Olympian Gods, moving puny humans around like pawns on their gameboards. You can date that back to the late 1800s, when Wilcox and White's organs, Thomas Edison's waxed cylinders, and the Aeolian Company's player pianos altered the course of music history.

My career has spanned a timeline of technology's planned obsolescence, with the production of vinyl albums, cassettes (ugh), eight-tracks (argh), CDs, and then digital files. In my role as a "recording artist," with contracts that defined me as such, I began to discover that technological layers of artifice, intended to enhance the listener's experience, can and sometimes miraculously do create their own kinds of truths. Yes — plural, actually — because recordings can have *layers*.

In Glenn Gould's life experience and his own way of thinking, the analog truth of recordings was superior to the original truth of music performed live.

*I get that.*

As a lifelong career musician, I can testify that digital technology made the process so much easier and far less expensive than it had ever been. In that, I can also completely agree with Mr. Byrne. The resultant biblical flood of music has levelled the field and removed almost all the hurdles that used to exist for common folks to become recording artists. Everyone with "voice memo" on their cellphone can be a fairly competent recording artist, with a product of decent quality. Anyone with a laptop and a software program (and access to the internet) can build upon loops and samples in a software program, build a website, and start a record label. Yes — it makes music "ubiquitous," which makes silence both rare and highly valued.

All true.

So why even bother to add to the flood? (This leads us back to the aesthetics of my tales.)

———•———

I'll give you four reasons why I wrote and played the music, and then described the entire process in this book:

1. Because I'm getting old. Music has been my life's career, and, as the "Winter Nocturne" tries to express, the inexpressible sadness of eternal silence is not too far off. So, I want to make a little more joyful noise, while I still can — and hope that the tales can get distributed and disseminated on a wider, simpler, more instantly-accessible basis than any live touring could accomplish. I've simply grown too old for the physical and mental demands of touring.

   Plus, I'm hoping that the optimism of my faith, hope, and love is also accessible in the tales — and even perceptible in the melancholy of "Winter Nocturne." And isn't it an extraordinary thing if a piece of written and recorded music can simultaneously carry layers of both my grief and joy of making music, informed by the three abiding graces, all in one track? In a live performance, I might aim for, but miss out on, delivering the heart of the matter. In a recording, I can at least do my level best to get as close to that truth as I possibly can, under the circumstances.

2. I still want to write and record because the technology is useful and convenient. Yes, a privileged white male from Burlington, Ontario, Canada might get judged from a distance as ripe for cancellation, a *has-been*. On the other side of that coin (always another perspective) this dude's been playing guitar for sixty-odd years, as a professional songwriter and recording artist for forty-eight of 'em. With a studio loft in his home, his

computer, software, and access to the internet — you never know — he *might* be qualified.

Oh, I've done enough committee work in academic and political situations to realize that the merits of meritocracy are often the very first babies that get tossed out with the dirty bathwater. And yes, for better or worse, digital technology makes it far too easy to cheat around the fundamentals of live performance chops. But a simple truth is — *I ain't dead yet.*

And I love making music.

3. Memoir writing brought the realization that I could write and record another kind of memoir, a musical one, circling back to the first pro-quality electric guitar I ever owned. Starting there, I could bring the tales right up to my present-tense state of affairs, and then write a book about it all.

That might provide an interesting set of challenges for a senior citizen.

4. For the pluralistic, humanistic, multi-faceted guy that the world fashioned me into, there are many truths, with many layers to those many truths. Here's a truth that The Beatles taught me when I was a teenager. In 1966, discouraged over and over again by the maniacal screaming hormones of their audience, as they vainly tried to deliver the natural truths of a live performance of their music — they retired from touring. That Which Cannot Be Preserved, floating in *that* air, was

mostly a disaster, sabotaged by another truth that was as undeniable as a biblical flood of another kind.

Ahh, but Abbey Road . . . the recording studio was offering a rapidly improving technological alternative, where creative work could take on all kinds of layers of meanings and emotional resonances and then be consumed by a listener in private, again and again, revealing itself in fresh, different ways. This was a truth on another plane of existence, and The Beatles made it work in glorious artistic ways that have yet to lose their vitality and charm.

— • —

In my lifetime, the evolution of recording arts and sciences was a miraculous development, giving rise to acts like Steely Dan — a band that served as a role model for me. Walter Becker and Donald Fagen were musicians who became "recording artists" in the highest aesthetic meaning of that term. Their amazingly great and sophisticated recordings became so much more than the surrounding "pop" offerings because they had deeply original compositions, married to their profound commitment for 'production' — arrangements, hiring the best sidemen, with the application of state-of-the-art technology for the highest audio quality possible in the recordings of their projects. Theirs were music recordings made for their own sake.

During this same period, rock bands like Led Zeppelin and Yes were heavily influential on me. They were also given free rein, with very healthy production budgets to indulge their creativity: not to sell singles, but *albums*.

Even though David Byrne is making a valid point about That Which Cannot Be Preserved, I feel there's an equally valid aesthetic argument to be made for That Which Should/Can/Must Be Preserved. As a recording artist himself, I feel confident that Mr. Byrne would agree.

Technology has surely been cannibalizing the value of music for the average person in the digital universe. Yes, modern digital economics have robbed recordings of their ability to earn a living for your average middle-of-the-pack recording artist. But just like me, recordings ain't dead yet, either. And, as far as I'm concerned, the recording can still maintain a truthful integrity that I still don't mind chasing after, from time to time.

Granted, That Which Cannot Be Preserved contains its own magical immunity for remaining alive and elusive and kicking arse. A good live musical performance offers folks a high-wire magical component, something that money can't buy — something that technological reproductions can't deliver.

Nevertheless, some predicted that TV would kill radio and the internet would kill publishing. Old delivery formats are shrinking, yes — yet somehow finding ways to survive within narrowing market demographic slices that prefer to get their truths in old-fashioned ways. For example, if I bother to manufacture vinyl albums, a thin market demographic is still eager to acquire them for their collections. There are still folks who enjoy a ritualized connoisseur experience.

And I'm still willing to take on the occasional side hustle.

As I remarked earlier in this book — Shakespeare didn't put future playwrights out of work: he just serves to (always) kick butt. And while Gutenberg's printing presses changed the world forever, so that the cultural institutions of oral tradition (and the readin' and writin' powers of The Church) were challenged by bookbinders, there are still truths that I can chase by offering my best efforts via the recording arts and crafts of 2024.

And here's yet another layer of truth: by writing this book about the Ten Telecaster Tales, I'm trying to get at the truth from another perspective. It's just another butt-kicking from a different angle.

Truth, like Love, requires the application of our own human elbow grease of Faith and Hope. Give it some of that, and you might discover that it can still ring true, in whatever form it appears.

I decided to put both hands in, right up to my elbows, at least one more time, and see what I could stir up. I made an old-fashioned album (albeit with some digital production trickery), and then wrote an old-fashioned book.

I still love playing guitar. I'm still half-decent at it. The recordings, for better or worse, are love's living proof.

There are still parts of me that don't feel much different than the kid I was when I first started playing. The **TEENAGER** who got his first **TELECASTER**. The **BAR BAND MUSICIAN** who heard **HIS SONG** on the radio for the first time. The **ROCK STAR** whose first solo album went **GOLD,** who designed his first **CUSTOM INSTRUMENT** and was inducted into **HALLS OF FAME** . . . (Please forgive showbiz escalations into *humblebrag*.)

Through all that, and so much more, my guitar has always been a trusty companion. It's always helped me cope with the negativities of this world, serving as a divining rod and leading me toward a keener sense of the truth.

———◄•►———

# "This Kind"

N 1996, I SAT DOWN IN MY BASEMENT STUDIO WITH MY
manager at the time, Ross Munro (who remains my very
dear friend), to play him a new song that I'd worked long, hard
days on and was really excited about. (Ahh, there it is again —
*the sin of pride*.)

After hearing "Taste of Steel," I could tell, immediately, that
Ross was torn right through the middle of his loving heart.
Gently, he said: "*Yeahhh* — Rikky, it's a great novelty song about
the joy of playing guitar, but (*pause for intake of breath and a
wince*) it'll never be the kind of song that finds commercial
success, especially in today's marketplace."

He asked me, "Just exactly what kind of artist do you want
to be?"

Good question.

Every choice, every decision that an artist makes in their career, in their life — that question provides a bottom line in the process. Here, now, in the third act of my life, as I sit and write memoir material, I've realized in retrospect that there were watershed tipping points — incidents and accidents on the timeline — that changed my particular history.

That moment with Ross was one of them.

At the ripe old age of forty-three, I was leaving behind the rock star I had been, and becoming . . . whatever and whoever it was I might turn into, down the road less travelled.

What kind of artist did I want to be?

I looked down at the guitar in my hands, and said . . .

"This kind."

> When this whole wide world around you gets unreal
> And you can't even say for sure the way you feel
> Well, then, you better make time for a genuine taste of steel . . .
>
> You let your fingers do the walkin' let the music do the talkin'
> You can spank it and tease it, caress it and squeeze it
> Well, you know without a doubt about the way you feel
> And your heart says, "Go ahead and make that deal,"
> On a genuine, certified, bona fide
> Taste of Steel.
>
> — RIK EMMETT, "TASTE OF STEEL," *Swing Shift* ALBUM (1997)

# ADDENDA

# 1

# Mix Notes For
# Ten Telecaster Tales

BY BLAIR PACKHAM, PROJECT ENGINEER

———————◆———————

Recorded at Eli's loft via iMac into Avid's Protools through an RME Fireface preamp/interface using a Shure SM57 to mic a Roland Cube 80 amp.

Mixed via M2 MacMini from MOTU Digital Performer 11 using a Universal Audio Apollo Quad 2 interface and Universal Audio (and other) plug-ins.

Universal Audio (UAD) plug-ins are noted for their faithful reproductions of much sought-after vintage gear and their simulations of actual studio environments and reverb chambers. Universal Audio, founded by legendary engineer/studio owner Bill Putnam, is a company that evolved from building high-end studio gear — mixers, pre-amps, compressors, et cetera, at a time when you couldn't just go to a store and buy that stuff — into an outfit that makes cutting-edge digital models of their own classic pieces, plus many other items from the golden age of recording.

Amongst those UAD items that we used, the Hitsville plug-ins are notable as re-creations of actual physical spaces (the reverb chambers in the attic) at the original Motown studio facility in Detroit. Also, the Ocean Way room is a model based on the actual dimensions of that famed LA studio and some of its legendary mic collection.

We also used plug-ins from Native Instruments, employing their Guitar Rig 6 simulator, not for its (excellent) amp models but for the models of classic effects units. Native Instruments also makes some excellent stand-alone modulation effects.

MOTU (Mark of the Unicorn) makes Digital Performer, the recording/mixdown/editing software we used for post-production; DP includes faithfully reproduced models of actual guitar stomp boxes, which we used here and there.

Almost all time-based modulation effects (rooms, reverbs, phasers, flangers, rotary speakers) were used sparingly in selected parts of the songs, literally, as an effect to enhance the emotional reaction a listener may have.

Frequency-based effects, like equalization, were mostly used in a set-and-forget way (for the whole song), in some cases to fix slight problems in the recording. (When recording a single instrument via a single microphone using the same settings for each song, certain problems may arise and are laid bare, depending on how hard or softly the guitar is played. To a large degree, we were able to address these problems subtly in the mixing process.)

A moment of serendipity occurred as we sought a tremolo/ vibrato effect for "Slinky." None of the standard plug-ins gave us what we wanted (a specific sound, like a Fender Rhodes Suitcase electric piano; a very *stereo* tremolo!). Leaning toward settling for something that was okay, we tried, without knowing what it would do, Native Instruments' FREAK (a not necessarily promising-sounding name). Instant gratification!

*Blair at the Neve console in*
*Union Sound Company, in Toronto.*

## So Pushy

Master Fader:
UAD Hitsville EQ Mastering model as hi-pass filter and
  to brighten at 2k, 5k, and 12.5k
UAD Hitsville Reverb Chamber 1 model as reverb
UAD Ocean Way room modeller as "reverb" using the
  Studio A/Guitar preset
UAD Roland Dimension D model used here and there

## Funky Scratchin'

UAD Ocean Way room modeller as "reverb" using the Studio
 A/Guitar preset, with hi-pass filter
NI Guitar Rig with Ensemble Chorus (like a Roland Jazz
 Chorus unit)
UAD Hitsville Reverb Chamber 1 model as reverb

## Swirling

UAD Ocean Way room modeller as "reverb" using the
 Studio A/Guitar preset
MOTU Analog Phaser (model of the original MXR Phase 90
 from the '70s)
MOTU ProVerb Large Hall as reverb (shorter)
UAD DreamVerb as reverb (longer)
NI FREAK as (very light) ring modulator/oscillator
 (via Guitar Rig)

## Allemande

Master Fader:
UAD Hitsville EQ model to roll off (slightly) at 50 Hz, 320
 Hz, and 800 Hz, and to boost (slightly) 130 Hz, 2000 Hz,
 and 12500 Hz
MOTU DeEsser to selectively compress 5 kHz where we
 had nail-scratching problems
UAD DreamVerb as long reverb
UAD Roland Dimension D model used here and there

MOTU Para EQ 2-band equalizer to lo-pass and hi-pass
Dimension D
UAD Hitsville Reverb Chamber 1 model as medium reverb

### Cowboy and Gaucho Waltz

Master Fader:
UAD Hitsville EQ Mastering model as hi-pass at 320 Hz
and to roll off at 12.5 kHz UAD Pultec EQP-1A model as
hi-pass at 100 Hz and to boost at 10 kHz
MOTU Dynamic Equalizer to selectively compress at 5 kHz
where we had nail-scratching problems, and boost at 11
kHz to brighten things up
UAD Hitsville EQ model to roll off at 50 Hz and 5000 Hz,
and to boost (slightly) 130 Hz
UAD Ocean Way room modeller as "reverb" using the
Studio A/Guitar preset, with hi-pass filter
MOTU Analog Flanger (model of an Electro-Harmonix
Electric Mistress)
MOTU AutoPan on the flanger return
MOTU ProVerb for a Large Hall reverb
UAD DreamVerb for a longer reverb

### Slinky

NI FREAK as (very light) ring modulator/oscillator
NI Tremolo (via Guitar Rig)
MOTU Para EQ 2-band equalizer (to get rid of an annoying
frequency being emphasized by the NI Tremolo) (−11 dB
at 130 Hz)

## BURLYTOWN

Master Fader:

UAD Hitsville EQ Mastering model as bass boost at 50 Hz and 130 Hz and to brighten at 2k and dip at 12.5 kHz

MOTU Dynamic Equalizer to selectively compress at 6 kHz where we had nail-scratching problems, and boost at 11 kHz to brighten things up

UAD Teletronix LA-2A Leveling Amplifier model, to lightly compress scratchy peaks

UAD Ocean Way room modeller as "reverb" using the Studio A/Guitar preset

NI Rotator Leslie-speaker effect (via Guitar Rig)

NI Guitar Rig with Ensemble Chorus (like a Roland Jazz Chorus unit)

UAD DreamVerb as shorter reverb

NI Replika digital delay (via Guitar Rig)


## THE RIO GLIDE

Master Fader:

UAD Hitsville EQ Mastering model as hi-pass filter and to brighten at 5k and 12.5 kHz

UAD DreamVerb as shorter reverb

NI Choral effect

NI Flanger/Chorus effect


## GEE WHIZ

UAD DreamVerb

Master Fader:

UAD Hitsville EQ Mastering model as hi-pass filter and to
brighten at 5k

MOTU Para EQ 2-band equalizer

(We rolled off everything below 250 Hz before sending it to
the effects; without this, the ambience sounded "boomy,"
"woofy," "fluffy," or other highly technical descriptors.)

UAD DreamVerb as long-ish reverb

NI Tape Echo (model of a classic Roland RE-201 Space Echo)
(via Guitar Rig)

NI Delay Man digital delay w. light chorus (model of an
Electro-Harmonix pedal) (via Guitar Rig)

(Both of these echo units only become active in the song's
bridge section, which is swimming in reverb, to give
depth and a dreamy effect.)

# 2

# Mastering Notes for Ten Telecaster Tales

## by Steve Skingley

———◆●▶———

MASTERING FOR THE RECORD TOOK PLACE AT NATURALLY Digital Mastering in Brampton, Ontario, on December 20, 2023, and January 19, 2024.

Rik talked to me about the idea of recording a series of electric guitar pieces back in August of 2023. He had been listening to different electric guitar players, like Joni Mitchell and Larry Carlton on *Hejira*, Bill Frisell, and Ed Bickert, and wanted to incorporate similar types of guitar effects and tones into his solo recordings. I thought this was a great idea and was excited to help him achieve the vision. Unfortunately, I wasn't available when Rik wanted to start tracking, so he enlisted his friend (and fantastic engineer), Blair Packham to record and mix.

When it came time for mastering, Rik reached out again and asked if I was up for the task.

I've always been impressed by Rik's loyalty to the people he enjoys working with. Many artists with the level of success Rik has achieved tend to go for a "big name" or a "hot new guy," which is understandable. But Rik seems to gravitate to people he likes and trusts. So, as neither a big name nor a hot new guy, I find it . . . refreshing.

I received the files a few days before the Christmas holidays and started the layout of the mastering session, which included importing all songs into my Pro Tools mastering template, measuring the tracks for loudness (in Integrated LUFS), and listening for general tone and frequency response. I also had a brief email exchange with Rik and Blair about any concerns or problems they wanted me to address.

I thought they'd done an incredible job. The compositions and performances were some of the best that I'd heard from Rik, and Blair had really nailed what I understood to be Rik's vision for the record, sonically. The only fixes to keep in mind were to control some "scratchiness" of Rik's acrylic nails hitting guitar strings on certain songs. I experienced the same thing during the recording and mixing of Rik's *Bonfire Sessions*, so I had some tools in mind that could help.

The first mastering session took place at Naturally Digital Mastering in Brampton, where the owner, Dave Vanderploeg, has an audiophile-level room outfitted with custom loudspeakers. I sometimes use an analog mastering chain at ND (which includes a very unique Buzz Audio optical compressor), but I wanted to keep things simple and 100 percent recallable, so I stayed completely in the box (all in the computer) for mastering. My main job was to raise levels, make the low end consistent-sounding across all songs, and tame some nail scratches on a couple of tracks.

The mastering chain consisted of the following plug-ins:

- Fab Filter ProQ 3 — for subtle low midrange corrections and dynamic midrange EQ. Hi-pass filter at 24hz.
- Kazrog K–Clip Clipper — adding level and subtle harmonic distortion — in Tube Mode.
- Lindell 80 Neve style channel strip — adding level. No EQ.
- UAD's Neve 33609 compressor — no compression, just adding some tone.
- Kazrog True Iron (transformer emulations) — adding level and some harmonic distortion.
- Fab Filter Saturn — adding some harmonic distortion — in Warm Tape mode (only on some tracks).
- Oeksound Soothe 2 — for taming midrange harshness.
- UAD's Oxford Inflator — adding level and some fullness. Clip Mode disengaged. Curve at full, effect level 12 percent.
- Fab Filter ProQ 3 — for low mid taming, dynamically.
- Oeksound Soothe 2 — for taming low mid and/or low end (only on some tracks).
- UAD's Pultec EQP 1-A — EQ cut and boost at 100hz & 5khz.

- Amek EQ200 Mastering EQ — subtle track-specific EQ & slight stereo widening — in MS Mode.
- Fab Filter Pro-L2 Limiter — final level adjustment and peak limiting.

Nail scratching artifacts were dealt with using a combination of a very narrow Q notch filter at 3.5 kHz (using the first Pro Q3 instance) and Soothe 2 set to target the same region. The first round of masters was received well by Rik and Blair, but they decided to do some mix revisions, so I went back to Naturally Digital on January 19 to make sure their fixes worked well with my mastering chains. Blair's mix updates were a definite improvement to tracks that already sounded great, so most of my original mastering stayed the same or very similar. (Hurray for 100 percent recallability!)

*Steve Skingley in the mastering room at*
*Naturally Digital Mastering in Brampton, Ontario.*

# Special Thanks

———— ◆ ————

T HEY SAY IT TAKES A VILLAGE, BUT IN THE CASE OF THIS project, it took four or five villages that surround me — protecting and aiding and abetting me.

In the circle of my village, I had Blair Packham and Steve Skingley to help me record an album (the thirty-second studio effort of my life) — and they both did stellar jobs. At the same time, I had been working with long-time collaborator Mike "Smitty" Smyth at MJS Custom Pickups, east of my Burlytown, over in west Mississauga. Nestled in between our villages, in Oakville, Garren Dakessian of Loucin Guitars built us Babs. These gentlemen are gurus and masters of their arts and crafts. I count on them to help me shape the sounds I hear in my imagination.

Then we reached out to Pittsburgh, PA, for the tried-and-true contributions of Jeanine Leech at Double Play Designs. Her illustrations on this project surpassed everything she's ever done (and she's done so much!) in the three decades we've worked together. For good and bad, she knows how I work and what I'm about — all the fusion of layers and styles and cross-fertilizing hybridization. She knows exactly what I mean when I write that her contribution to creative vision struck *Steampunk Gold*!

*Ten Telecaster Tales* required vision and leadership from the ECW Press camp, provided with grace and intelligence by

Michael Holmes and his own MisFit label. He conscripted Victoria Cozza and Jessica Albert, and after Editorial finished with my beautiful mess, things moved over to Emily Ferko for sales and Claire Pokorchak for publicity. *Ten Telecaster Tales* marks our third adventure in the marketplace together.

The somewhat unusual coupling of record with book required villagers who could perform the role of parts assembly and market fulfillment. With grateful relief, we villagers called upon Greg Ross and Myk Rudnick down at Manic Merch in Syracuse, New York.

For a few decades, I have enjoyed the support and consideration of Larry Davidson at D'Addario Canada. Their strings grace every guitar in Eli's Loft, providing an integral contribution to my music making.

Thank you all for aiding and abetting this storyteller in his latest round of tales. I couldn't have done it without you.

Before there were 194 pages of liner notes for a guitar and its music, there were ten songs. Ten tunes that were instrumental electric guitar pieces: Ten Telecaster Tales. Now, if your journey through these pages has piqued your curiosity about what those songs actually *sound* like, you can find them here:

https://rikemmett.bandcamp.com/

...where you can preview them, and if you're of a certain mind, you can up the ante and download them from there. I assure you, the storyteller who wrote and recorded those tales on his trusty guitar named Babs would be mighty grateful.

**Entertainment. Writing. Culture.** ────────────

ECW is a proudly independent, Canadian-owned book publisher. We know great writing can improve people's lives, and we're passionate about sharing original, exciting, and insightful writing across genres.

──────────────────────── **Thanks for reading along!**

We want our books not just to sustain our imaginations, but to help **Certified** construct a healthier, more just world, and so we've become a certified B Corporation, meaning we meet a high standard of social and environmental responsibility — and we're going to keep aiming higher. We believe books can drive change, but the way we make them can too.

**Corporation**

Being a B Corp means that the act of publishing this book should be a force for good — for the planet, for our communities, and for the people that worked to make this book. For example, everyone who worked on this book was paid at least a living wage. You can learn more at the Ontario Living Wage Network.

This book is also available as a Global Certified Accessible™ (GCA) ebook. ECW Press's ebooks are screen reader friendly and are built to meet the needs of those who are unable to read standard print due to blindness, low vision, dyslexia, or a physical disability.

The interior of this book is printed on Sustana EnviroBook™, which is made from 100% recycled fibres and processed chlorine-free.

**FSC**
www.fsc.org
**MIX**
Paper | Supporting responsible forestry
**FSC® C016245**

ECW's office is situated on land that was the traditional territory of many nations including the Wendat, the Anishnaabeg, Haudenosaunee, Chippewa, Métis, and current treaty holders the Mississaugas of the Credit. In the 1880s, the land was developed as part of a growing community around St. Matthew's Anglican and other churches. Starting in the 1950s, our neighbourhood was transformed by immigrants fleeing the Vietnam War and Chinese Canadians dispossessed by the building of Nathan Phillips Square and the subsequent rise in real estate value in other Chinatowns. We are grateful to those who cared for the land before us and are proud to be working amidst this mix of cultures.

ecwpress.com